DIGITAL LEARNING

The new edition of *Digital Learning: The Key Concepts* is the perfect reference for anyone seeking to navigate the myriad of named concepts, approaches, issues and technologies associated with digital learning.

Key terms are explained succinctly, making this book ideal to dip into for a quick answer, or to read from cover-to-cover, in order to gain a mastery of how digital concepts fit within the world of education. Fully updated to include important developments in digital practice and technology in education over the last ten years, this book takes the reader from A to Z through a range of relevant topics including:

- Course design
- Digital scholarship
- Learning design
- Open education
- Personal learning environments
- Social media and social networking.

Ideal as an introductory guide, or as a reference book for ongoing referral, this quick-to-use and comprehensive guide is fully cross-referenced and complete with suggestions for further reading and exploration, making it an essential resource for anyone looking to extend their understanding of digital practices, techniques and pedagogic concepts.

Frank Rennie is a Professor and Assistant Principal at Lews Castle College of the University of the Highlands and Islands, UK.

Keith Smyth is Professor of Pedagogy and Head of the Learning and Teaching Academy at the University of the Highlands and Islands, UK.

Digital Learning: The Key Concepts provides a valuable reference for education professionals, particularly early-career Learning Technologists, academics and teachers getting to grips with the intersection between digital technology and education. The clear explanations give a rapid orientation within the ideas and terminology of this important aspect of the contemporary learning landscape.

Antony Coombs, Learning Technologies Manager (Technology Enhanced Learning), University of Sussex, UK

Navigating the constantly evolving digital learning landscape is a perennial challenge for staff, students and indeed anyone involved in any type of learning activity. This updated collection of terms provides an essential compass for key learning theories, concepts and resources for navigating the current digital learning landscape.

Sheila MacNeill, Senior Lecturer in Digital Learning, Glasgow Caledonian University, UK

As someone working in education who is also studying digital learning as part of a postgraduate qualification, this book is invaluable as a quick reference guide for key concepts in digital learning and also key concepts relevant to wider learning and teaching contexts. I would recommend that anyone studying or involved in digital education has *Digital Learning: The Key Concepts* by their side as a reference guide.

Alex Walker, Professional Recognition and Development Coordinator, University of the Highlands and Islands, UK

DIGITAL LEARNING

The Key Concepts

Second Edition

Frank Rennie and Keith Smyth

Routledge
Taylor & Francis Group

LONDON AND NEW YORK

Second edition published 2020
by Routledge
2 Park Square, Milton Park, Abingdon, Oxon, OX14 4RN

and by Routledge
52 Vanderbilt Avenue, New York, NY 10017

Routledge is an imprint of the Taylor & Francis Group, an informa business

British Library Cataloguing-in-Publication Data
A catalogue record for this book is available from the British Library

Library of Congress Cataloging-in-Publication Data
Names: Rennie, Frank author. | Mason, Robin. E-learning.
Title: Digital learning : the key concepts / Frank Rennie and Keith Smyth.
Other titles: E-learning
Description: Second Edition. | New York : Routledge, 2020. | Originally published: London ; New York : Routledge, 2006, under title E-learning / by Robin Mason and Frank Rennie.
Identifiers: LCCN 2019007290| ISBN 9781138353701 (Hardback) | ISBN 9781138353732 (Paperback) | ISBN 9780429425240 (Ebook)
Subjects: LCSH: Internet in education. | Computer-assisted instruction. | World Wide Web.
Classification: LCC LB1044.87 .M27 2020 | DDC 371.33/44678–dc23
LC record available at https://lccn.loc.gov/2019007290

ISBN: 978-1-138-35370-1 (hbk)
ISBN: 978-1-138-35373-2 (pbk)
ISBN: 978-0-429-42524-0 (ebk)

Typeset in Bembo
by Swales & Willis, Exeter, Devon, UK

CONTENTS

FIGURES

LIST OF KEY CONCEPTS

Accessibility
Active learning
Activity-based learning
Affordances
Agent
Andragogy
Animations
App
Artificial intelligence
Assessment
Asynchronous learning
Attachment
Audio/video clips
Audioconference
Augmented reality
Authentication
Avatar

Bandwidth
Behaviourism
Bit/byte
Bite-sized learning
Blended learning
Blogging (weblogging)
Bluetooth
Brainstorming
Bring your own device
Broadband
Browser
Case study
Chatroom/chatbox

Client
Cloud computing
Cognitivism
Collaborative work/learning
Community of inquiry
Community open online course (COOC)
Communities
Computer-based training (CBT)
Computer conferencing
Connectivism
Constructivism
Content aggregation
Content curation
Convergence
Cookie
Copyright
Course design
Courseware
Creative Commons
Cyberspace
Cyberstalking

Data security
Database
Desktop
Digital badge
Digital divide
Digital literacy
Digital natives and immigrants
Digital scholarship

Digital university
Digital visitors and residents
Digitizing
Discussion board
Distributed education
Domain name
Domain of one's own (DoOO)
Download
Dropbox

ECDL (European
  Computer Driving Licence)
Edutainment
Email
Emoticons
Encryption
Eportfolio
E-textbooks
Experiential learning

Face-to-face (f2f)
Facebook
Facilitator
FAQs
Feedback
File transfer protocol (ftp)
Firewall
Flaming (or flame war)
Flexible learning
Folksonomy

Gamification
Gif
Graphics
Groupwork

Hacker
Hardware
Hashtag
Helpline/helpdesk
Heutagogy
Homepage

HTML
HTTP
Hyper-interactivity
Hyperlink/hypertext

Icon
ICT
Instant messaging
Instructional design
Interaction
Internet
Internet café
Internet of things (IOT)
Internet service provider (ISP)
Intranet

Java
JPEG

Killer app

LAN (local area network)
Laptop
Learning design
Learning management system
  (LMS)
Learning objects
Lifelong learning
Logon/off or login/out
Lurking

Mentoring
Meta tag
Metadata
Micro-blogging
Micro-credentialing
MLE
Mobile learning
Modem
Moderator
Module
MOOC (massive open online
  course)

Motivation
Multimedia
Multiple choice question (MCQ)

Netiquette
Networks

Online
Online libraries
Open access
Open dataOpen educational
   practice
Open educational resources
   (OER)Open learning
Open source
Open textbook

Password
PDF
Pedagogy
Peer assessment
Peer-to-peer
Personal learning environment
   (PLE)
Personal learning network (PLN)
Plagiarism
Platform
Podcast
Post or posting
Problem-based learning (PBL)

QR codes
Quality assurance

Retention
Reusing, reworking and remixing
Role play
RSS

Screen dump
Search engine
Self-directed learning
Semantic Web
Serious games

Server
Simulation
Situated learning
Skype
Smartphone
Snail mail
Social bookmarking
Social capital
Social media
Social networking
Social presence
Software
Spam
Stack Exchange
Stalking
Student-centred learning/
   learner-centred learning
Surfing
Synchronous learning

Tablet
Tagging
Text messaging
Threaded discussion
Toolbar
Trojan
TrollTrust
Tutor group
Tutor marked assignment (TMA)
Tutoring
Tweet
Twitter

Upload
URL

Validation
Videoconferencing
Virtual reality
Virtual seminar
Virtual university
Virus

VLE
Vodcast

Web
Web 2.0
Web-based learning
Web enabled
Web feed
Web presence
Webcam
Webcast
Webinar
Weblog

Webpage
WebQuests
Welcome page
Wi-fi
Wiki
Wikipedia
Wireless network
Worm

YouTube

XML

PREFACE TO THE 2019 EDITION

If 'a week is a long time in politics', then thirteen years is almost an era in educational technology. Since the first edition of this book was published in 2006, there have been huge changes, in software, hardware, practices, and attitudes towards education in an online environment, and more broadly regarding the use of digital technologies and resources within learning and teaching. Much of the terminology remains relevant, but in addition to a new vocabulary emerging, some of the older words are evolving a new meaning. Terms such as 'social presence' have acquired a wider relevance, and a recognition of greater importance, than simply having a tutor or a buddy to contact online. Events such as videoconferencing have ceased to become a vision from a sci-fi future and have become incorporated into public and private life, with services such as Skype for Business and FaceTime available for personal computing devices and smartphones. The phenomenon of social media has arrived, spilled over from a recreational activity into the sphere of formal interactivity, and is now used daily in educational exchanges, in business meetings, and to support communication and collaboration within geographically and digitally dispersed groups and communities.

The apparent ubiquity of devices that connect us to each other through the internet has diversified them and made them more affordable to individuals. No industry expert predicted the astonishing growth in importance of SMS text messages, nor the pervasive influence of micro-blogging on Twitter as a tool of social and political discourse. Nor is it clear, despite the many potential opportunities for development, where the next 'big thing' may take us. The only certainty is that anyone who claims to be able to predict the future is almost surely wrong.

Despite that, there are a number of generic threads that are unlikely to disappear, however vague and/or overwhelming the future of educational technology might seem. Firstly, the astonishing growth in the availability of online education has made it almost omnipresent. There is scarcely any university across the globe that does not engage with digital resources for education in one form or another. In some institutions, entire degree programmes and research schools are primarily online. Hundreds of other institutions favour a blended model, with an almost infinite variety of mixtures combining face-to-face communications with online activities, support or resources. Even some traditionally conservative subjects, which require practical instruction, field experience, or hands-on learning activities, now incorporate online education to provide lecture-capture, online libraries or non-synchronous networked learning activities to back up the face-to-face experience.

The spectacular growth of the World Wide Web, and multi-directional Web 2.0 in particular, has produced a seemingly limitless array of digital resources that can be utilised for learning and teaching in every field of human knowledge. Video clips, images, text, audio recordings, animations, live interactive sessions and archived data are now available with only a few clicks (and perhaps a registered user id and password). Having said that, many digital educational resources are increasingly freely available to use and adapt, having been produced and published under open licences. Within the wider field of digital open education that has emerged in recent years, the sector has also seen the development and subsequent proliferation of large-scale open online courses (MOOCs), through which many universities are offering free online learning opportunities. Various open textbook initiatives are also committed to the development and distribution of free online textbooks for college and university students. Similarly, for academics, open access journals and digital scholarship practices are changing the ease and immediacy with which research, scholarship and scholarly dialogue can be disseminated and engaged.

In our own work and practice, we have both been closely involved in various open education initiatives, in the creation and analysis of many of digital education resources, and in designing and facilitating online programmes of study and open learning opportunities. Of course, there is a lot of nonsense and incorrect information on the web, just as there is in offline life, but there is also copious information of the very highest quality and the most up-to-the-moment currency. Making sense of all of this, including the myriad of formal and informal networks and learning opportunities that are now available, requires a new literacy, a new awareness, and new technical abilities on the part of both learners and educators.

In preparing the second edition of this book, we have not tried to second-guess the future. There will be other occasions more appropriate for doing that. In addition, while we have expanded our coverage of relevant educational concepts and positions, we have not attempted to offer any detailed evaluation of the merits of different pedagogical processes. Instead, we take the view that while effective learning can be supported in a range of ways there is a need to recognise that the tools and means for communicating with learners (formal and non-formal), for connecting learners with each other, and for accessing relevant educational resources are changing and require a better understanding.

For this new edition, we have also provided a new introduction, although we have opted to cover the finer detail of the current digital learning landscape across the updated and expanded range of concepts, issues, approaches and technologies we cover in the main body of the book. However, the key point from both the original induction to the first edition and our new introduction remains unchanged. There are some aspects that require reconsideration, but, fundamentally, the message is the same. There is no magic formula. The technology should not dominate the learning; the key point is that the needs of the learner should come first, and the technologies should be adopted/adapted to ensure that the learning experience is successful as a quality collaboration.

The main part of this book has been updated to acknowledge the shift in terminology over the last dozen years. The new additions are sometimes just as surprising as the terms that remain unchanged; 'Twitter' and 'Tweet' have crept into our normal conversation, but it is apparently just as relevant as ever to explain what bandwidth is. Those familiar with the first edition of this book will perhaps have noticed one significant change in terminology: the replacement of 'elearning' with 'Digital Learning' in the title of the new edition, to reflect the broader range of relevant concepts, practices and approaches that the latter term has come to encompass in recent years.

This book is intended for the learner who is a newcomer to using technology to enhance learning, for students of education and digital learning, and for the educator who seeks new ways of enhancing and supporting the learning experience that they facilitate. Each term explains words that are encountered in the pursuit of education in an online environment. The words in **bold** cross-refer to other definitions in this book. We attempt to be systematic and logical, but we make no claims to being comprehensive. The language continues to change with the evolution of the subject matter and the sophistication of the average user. Twenty years ago, 'getting online' was the indulgence of a relative few; now, grandparents regularly speak with their grandchildren across the world and learn what they have been doing in the past week, and self-motivated learners seek out the resources that they need, regardless of the availability of a suitable local course or tutor. This does not mean, of course, that everybody who uses digital technology for learning is able to utilise the most appropriate tools in the best manner. Learning to learn is a skill, and, like any other skill, it needs to be nurtured. Hopefully, this book will help to dispel some of the professional jargon associated with educational technology and, in doing so, will make learning more enjoyable and more meaningful.

For those who need more (and there are always some) we have tried to supply, at the end of this book, a list of useful further reading, websites and sources of support. We are conscious that this list is brief, subjective and time-limited. There will always be more that could be said. The intention of this book is to prepare the ground for online explorations in greater detail, both for students and for tutors. The last words are that we, too, are learning something new every day. Enjoy.

Professor Frank Rennie
Professor Keith Smyth
University of the Highlands and Islands, Scotland.

ACKNOWLEDGEMENTS

The first edition of this book was co-written with Professor Robin Mason, of the UK Open University, who passed away soon after the publication. Her enthusiasm, dry humour and commitment to enhancing online education continues to inspire all those who worked with her.

We would also like to extend our sincere gratitude and thanks to Antony Coombs, Sheila MacNeill and Alex Walker for taking the time to review the content of this second edition and for their very helpful suggestions for additional key concepts and terms for inclusion. We also thank the aforementioned for kindly providing their endorsements of the text for potential readers. We are also indebted to the Routledge team, who supported us in bringing this second edition together, not least for their very timely and valuable input at each stage of production and publication.

INTRODUCTION

In the introduction to the first edition of this book, the opening sentence drew attention to the inadvisability of attempting to predict the future of elearning. That was good advice, for no one could have accurately foretold the changes in the educational technology sector over the thirteen years since the first edition was published. In this time, whole concepts have disappeared, or at least faded from significance to such an extent that the terms look jaded and dated. Many 'accepted' beliefs have been challenged, overturned, revised, adapted or have re-emerged in response to different ways of attempting to utilise technology. In particular, internet-related technology has blossomed for education and training. Future possibilities will prove to be equally surprising and exciting, but for now let's stick to what we know from the past decade and a half.

If we ignore for the moment the technology issues themselves – the fact that devices have become smaller, more affordable, more interconnected and more mobile – there have been three major trends in education that is available in the digital environment.

Firstly, social media has burst on the scene. In education and in work, as in our personal lives, it may sometimes appear that we operate in a permanently interconnected environment. Any ad hoc survey in an airport, or a commuter train, or a shopping mall, or indeed anywhere that crowds gather, will be certain to record a high proportion of individuals staring at their smartphones or tablets. The ability to almost instantaneously share digital information with friends and relatives has resulted in a burgeoning of digital communications in all the usual areas of human society. There are open and closed networks where people share romantic information, and there are hate groups; there are specialist networks in virtually all areas of academic study and in most hobbies, whether football, stamp collecting or simply admiring particular breeds of pets. The ease of communication in this new media has simultaneously accelerated the importance of collaboration in highly intricate sciences and in global journalism, and at the same time it has trivialised information to an absurd level, where millions seem obsessed with posting pictures of their food or of the traffic accident that they have just witnessed.

It seems natural that social media has been explored for use in education, but the results have sometimes been unexpected. Concerns over the security of information shared, as well as with attaining the appropriate level of formality for structured learning, have been well-reflected in the academic literature. Both of these concerns change with the evolving cultural norm of wider society, and no doubt diverse educational structures will continue to experiment and adapt. On the other hand, the ability of social media to level the communications platform has apparently contributed significantly to the democratisation of education. This is noticeable both in the sense of giving value to other voices or views and in enabling wider access for a different demography of learners than was common throughout the twentieth century. Social media is still growing and evolving, and it almost goes without saying that the momentum is so strong that we will see many more innovations and applications of social media to education in the next decade or two. The big unanswered question of this moment is, to what extent can social media be adopted for use in a formal educational setting? Many of us have seen from experience that while students are comfortable using social media for chatting among their peers, they are not necessarily at ease when asked to use it for structured learning. There are a whole range of issues to be considered, including the use of correct academic language, the professional distance between student and tutor, netiquette, plagiarism and the security of private conversations which pass through a third-party software supplier.

There is no doubt that social media, in all its emerging formats (and others to be discovered) can play an important role in networking the global communities of learners and educators. The current problem is that the technological ability is so new, and so much faster and more pervasive than previous forms of networking, that society is still on a steep learning curve as to what what could and should – and should not – be common operational practices. Is it best for social media to be constrained to a support role for learners, rather than as a medium of instruction or tuition, or can the functionality of social media software be brought 'in-house' to shelter within the protected digital environment of the global university? Certainly, branding and reputation are seen to be a key factor in persuading viewers to 'follow' the work of particular individuals and institutions, and perhaps we might see the development of a meritocracy for classifying digital resources along the lines of the recommendation rubrics of Amazon or eBay. On the other hand, it has become a common feature in the daily news to comment on fake websites, internet scams and identity theft, so there is still some way to go to replicate the security of a personal appearance.

This raises the second major trend in digital education – increasing openness. Since the early days of the UK Open University, there has been a steady spread and enhancement of open educational resources. It was a natural extension of the philosophy to broaden 'open educational resources' into the digital world as well as the developing structures of paper-based and conference-call resources. Openness is covered in several different reference definitions in this book because there are multiple facets of openness. From open source programming, which shares the raw code, to open access journals making academic articles easier to find and read, to open textbooks that are a direct attempt to democratise the economics of learning, the field of 'openness' is mushrooming. The philosophy is more complicated than it might seem at first, because who pays for the 'free' resources? Ultimately, even if we only give up our free time to create and curate those resources, there is a cost somewhere. There are several variations of dealing with the apparent paradox surrounding the economics of providing free educational resources. Some journals, for instance, charge authors upfront to publish their articles, in order to make the cost free to users later. Other journals defray the costs among volunteer reviewers, editors and allied services. Yet other institutions offer free resources as an enticement to encourage users to sign up (and pay) for a more extensive range of resources, and perhaps for structured tutorials, assessment, and so on.

Furthermore, we are currently witnessing the emergence of critical narratives and debates that are urging a reframing of open education so that it is not, as has become the general case, associated mainly with 'open online' but instead encompasses considerations of 'open on campus' and 'open in the community', including the role digital technologies and spaces can play in supporting an intersection of open education practices, locations and approaches.

Whatever the paradigm, there is little doubt that an open access search for information is the first choice for many, if not most, and to 'Google it' is a phrase that has entered common parlance. In a similar manner to the growth of social media, the ability to instantly connect with open digital resources such as journals, archives, videos, data and relevant networks of like-minded users has become a phenomenon which users take for granted. Although the ability to access information openly online is not ubiquitous, and is still patchy for many subject areas, the facility has already dramatically influenced the educational and research behaviours of many researchers. For the new generation of postgraduate students, open access information is an expectation, not simply a hope, and in response to these demands it is driving us to experiment with new ways of sharing resources with peers.

An inevitable consequence of enhanced digital social networks and increasing open access to high-quality educational resources online is the higher status being accorded to self-determined learning. Following a historical trend, from a formal education that was highly structured and tightly prescribed what students must learn, through a more open structure that laid emphasis on 'just-in-time' learning according to student need, the latest iteration is heutagogy. While pedagogy techni-cally refers to the methods and practice of education with children, and andragogy relates to adult learning, heutagogy encourages self-determined learning that places the student at the centre of the learning process. In this theoretical perspective, the role of the tutor is to help share knowledge, to direct students to appropriate learning resources that match their needs and, rather than to 'teach' students, to help them to learn how to learn independently. This is a concept of education that can probably trace its roots back to Socrates but which reaches its apogee in the facilitation of internet-based, open access, digital educa-tional resources. The tutors use their expert knowledge to draw together a wide range of high-quality resources which the students can study independently, or not at all. The skill and the experience of the tutor becomes a form of quality benchmark, which can indicate to learners the importance, the direction and the relevance of individual educational resources in understanding the epistemology of the subject which is being studied. In an online, digital environment, the digital element enables a high level of fidelity in replication of resources, while also enabling easy repurposing; the online element enables global networking to link learners with scholars and other students.

The potential mixture of approaches to learning in the medium of online digital communications is immense. Combining audio recordings, video clips, discussion boards, live webinars, online libraries and image banks, and many other digital resources (see Rennie and Morrison, 2013) offers almost limitless opportunities to provide educational experience. For this reason, many online courses are underpinned by the constructivism theory of learning, where knowledge of the world is literally built, or constructed, by adding new experiences and mental models to that which we already know. Such models can start simply, as with a child starting playgroup, and aggregate over time to become increasingly complex and sophisticated. The almost limitless access to new ideas, data and evidence which can be shared in the digital educational environment is a powerful resource to support constructivist learning. Many educationalists argue the need for a tutor, or a facilitator of learning, in order to systematise these learning experiences and to provide an epistemological framework with which to order and to prioritise the relevance of the disparate resources, but this too can be accommodated in the digital learning environment. In addition to the use of technology to connect learners and tutors, the use of online learning resources is not confined only to online engagement, and various hybrid combinations of online/offline activities have been labelled 'blended learning' (although this term is often misused as a generic 'catch-all').

From a theoretical perspective, constructivism and constructivist learning theories continue to provide the main conceptual lenses, models, principles and perspectives for framing digital learning practice, scholarship and research. A more recent concept is connectivism, which emphasises the non-linear ability of digital networks to make multiple connections to enhance learning and which places the value of the ability to learn in the strength of those connections. As a concept, it is still too early to tell if 'connectivism' is a unique theory of learning or simply a useful way to view the practical application of constructivism, but the concept has introduced new ways of thinking about access to digital learning resources, including MOOCs and COOCs as well as other network approaches to learning.

As the application of digital resources to education has become easier and almost ubiquitous, our conceptual and theoretical perspectives have deepened and extended their scope. This has also helped to enhance our understanding of offline education, and the contrasts between the two approaches have frequently been demonstrated to be less about technology and more about the application of new communications opportunities to established educational theories. New ideas have emerged from a more nuanced focus on research opportunities provided by the increased interest in using digital resources (and services) for learning, and this strengthened research base has in turn furthered our understanding of the underpinning theories.

To explore just one strand by way of explanation: new abilities to speedily communicate with widely distributed networks of learners, and therefore stimulate many-to-many learning experiences, reduced geographical and time constraints, but they initially raised some concerns about the provision of support services to reduce learners' feelings of isolation. This led to a greater appreciation of how digital resources can provide more than simply tutor-student exchanges, with a blossoming range of other opportunities to enable access to services such as online libraries, study guides, peer-to-peer learning and digital pastoral care. As in face-to-face education, there is no 'one-size-fits-all' for the provision of digital online learners, and this led to the increasing importance of recognising social presence, personal identity and personal choice in learning environments. As these issues grew in significance – each complex, interrelated and context-dependent – so too did the awareness of being able to, to some extent, 'customise' educational experiences in order to fine-tune the personal learning environment to emphasise student-centred learning. The flexibility of distributed, open, offline education is magnified in the online environment, with multiple opportunities to access, interrogate and share digital resources – including the knowledge of other learners and educators – across the planet.

The evolving research base for digital learning has also expanded in recent years to establish our current understanding of digital literacies and capabilities (e.g. Goodfellow and Lea, 2013), supporting a more critical exploration of the specific affordances of different educational technologies (Evans et al., 2017), and to provide evidence relating to digitally supported collaborative learning, learning in virtual worlds, adaptive learning environments, self-regulated learning and digital divides (e.g. as covered through the contributions to Duval et al., 2017).

We are now at a stage in the provision of education when older forms of engagement with Higher Education sit cheek-by-jowl with forms that are so new they have barely been tested in earnest. In between, there is a plethora of digital resources, communication opportunities and forms of educational engagement, which the digital university is challenged to adopt and adapt. Indeed, the concept of what a 'Digital University' is, or should be, has also emerged as an area of research and debate within the Higher Education sector (Johnston et al., 2019).

In the larger educational milieu, digital opportunities for learning are multiplying in Primary and Secondary schools, in the workplace and in non-formal, self-directed learning. Undoubtedly, our thinking will change many times in the next few years as our understanding of this global digital educational environment evolves, but neither educators nor learners can afford to ignore or look on from the edges. This book is an attempt to raise the bar of awareness, to challenge the current understanding and to encourage a more informed critical appreciation of the potential of digital educational practices, resources and technologies.

KEY CONCEPTS

ACCESSIBILITY

In terms of elearning, accessibility generally has two specific meanings. Computer accessibility refers to the usability of a computer system for individual users. This would cover disabilities such as colour blindness, dyslexia, sound impairment and lack of manual dexterity. **Web** accessibility generally refers to the increasingly common practice of making pages on the **internet** accessible to all users, regardless of whether they access via a slow **modem** or a state-of-the-art **broadband** connection. An example is large files or complex **graphics** that may be impossible to **download** without a high-**bandwidth** connection, resulting in the 'freezing' of the system and frustration to the potential user. The key to a consideration of accessibility is to enable users to access information in their own preferred manner, and so this is closely related to the thoughtful design of **distributed education**. In making computers and the web accessible, careful planning can enhance usability for all users, not just those with specific disabilities. Examples are that some users may prefer text links rather than **icons**, while the incorporation of sound files to accompany images does not simply benefit users with a visual impairment. The ability for individual users to self-select the level of accessibility required, for example for a colour-blind user to select a particular colour scheme on the screen, is a feature that is increasingly being built into public-access internet sites.

ACTIVE LEARNING

This concept refers to techniques where students do more than simply listen to a lecture. The notion is not new and not a product of elearning. However, it has been given added impetus through elearning, which is strongly associated with many forms of active learning: **constructivism, self-directed learning, interaction** and those processes which engage the learner in an active rather than passive mode.

Adapting active learning to the **online** environment usually involves dialogue with the teacher or other learners, observing or taking part in **case studies, role plays** or **simulations**. There is often resistance to active learning by students who are accustomed to lectures or students who prefer passive learning. It is important therefore to prepare students by explaining the objectives of active learning and offering support in the initial stages.

ACTIVITY-BASED LEARNING

This is not a precisely defined term and is usually thought of in opposition to passive learning. It marks a shift away from content-based learning which is associated with lectures and some forms of distance education. The underlying theory is that people learn by doing and that experience is the basis of all learning. Allied with the element of activity is the notion of reflection, and together these two components form a cyclic process: action and reflection on action.

AFFORDANCES

The term 'affordance' has come to refer to what different technologies offer by way of their specific educational benefits. For example, asynchronous **discussion boards** allowing learners more time to think and reflect before offering their views, or a visual **simulation** which allows a learner to study a process or procedure in a more realistic way than static pictures.

However, this general use of the term 'affordance' is a problematic one as it assumes the educational benefits that a particular technology might offer are there to be realised by every learner that interacts with that technology. The reality is a more complex one.

The concept of 'affordances' was originally conceived by the ecological psychologist James Gibson, in the 1970s. Gibson used the term 'affordance' to describe the 'emergent' relationship between the individual and the opportunities for action offered by objects in their environment. For example, a pen affording the opportunity to write, but predicated firstly on the individual recognising that the object is indeed a pen and could be used for written communication and, secondly, on the individual having a need to write.

Applying this more nuanced original perspective to educational technologies, we can recognise that an asynchronous discussion board may well offer more time to reflect and debate, leading to deeper learning, and may offer less outgoing learners further time and space to engage with peers. However, this is only so if the learner recognises these features and does not engage with a discussion board for the first time immediately before it closes and when they can, at best, only quickly communicate their own views. Similarly, a visual simulation will offer less to a learner who passively watches or interacts the simulation than to a learner who studies the content of the simulation until they have understood what is depicted.

There is ongoing debate concerning the affordances of educational technologies, and continued variation in whether the term is being used as a general one or being applied more critically in line with Gibson's original theory (for example, Evans et al., 2017). Arguably, the more useful perspective is of affordances as 'emergent' properties, rather than existing simply to be received and experienced. This view also points towards the need to ensure that learners are well supported to understand how to use different technologies effectively for educational purposes, beyond knowing how to operate or interact with them technically.

A more nuanced view of affordances would also acknowledge that learners with specific **accessibility** requirements are supported, including through assistive technologies, to have a comparable and equitable experience using the same or similar technologies to their peers.

AGENT

A particular type of **software** application designed in such a way that it can take a variety of 'decisions' based upon the design constraints of its programmers. Agents have been used to create the appearance of a person with whom the user can have different levels of **interaction** and carry out a number of basic tasks or enquiries. At least one European university has used a sophisticated agent to create a **helpline** 'problem page' facility by introducing new students to the 'character' of their agent who can 'discuss' with other students a range of study problems and possible solutions. A measure of the success of this agent is that several students have apparently attempted to date her!

ANDRAGOGY

The theory and practice of helping adults learn (as distinct from **pedagogy**, which, though widely used in teaching, actually refers specifically to helping children learn). Andragogy explicitly recognises that adults have different skills and experiences than young children, and therefore often require slightly different priorities for learning. The high proportion of adults engaging in **online learning** frequently encourages a continuum between andragogy and **heutagogy**, particularly with the growing access to **open educational resources** on the **web.**

Leading proponents of andragogy include Malcolm Knowles, who developed a theory of adult learning based on principles such as the need for adult learners to be involved in planning and evaluating their educational activities. Experience and **experiential learning** as a basis for learning and knowledge development is also important, as is ensuring the relevance of educational activities to the needs and interests of adult learners. In drawing a distinction between andragogy and heutagogy, many theorists and practitioners align andragogy with self-directed learning and heutagogy with self-determined learning.

ANIMATIONS

These are moving drawings that can be used to illustrate sequential stages in a process (e.g. a flow diagram of a project) or give the impression of moving parts (e.g. a schematic diagram of how a car engine operates). Animations can be used in combination with text, sound and **hyperlinks** to create a rich **online** learning environment that improves on simple text and/or still photographs on a printed page. Complex or interlinked animations can be used to create a **network** of special effects that can be used to illustrate events online where **video clips** are not possible or appropriate. An example of this is the illustration of the geological sequence of the movement of the continents into their present position available at http://highered.mheducation.com/sites/0072402466/student_view0/chapter15/animations_and_movies.html#. Animations are created by drawing a series of images of an object and making small changes to each image to simulate movement. The greater the number of individual images to a movement, then the smoother the apparent transition will be. Animations have been used on CDs as a learning resource in **distributed education**, and as more users gain access to higher **bandwidth** over the **internet** (such as **broadband**) then it becomes easier to incorporate animations in **webpages** or the managed learning environment (**MLE**). An obstacle to their use over lower bandwidths is that the large number of images required for very detailed animations produces large, complex files that move very slowly (if at all) on slow data transmission lines. As an example, compare the moving image of Gondwanaland at https://karto web.itc.nl/gondwana/gondwana.html. This is a large and complex file, so it will require a fast **web** access. Animations are ideal for online tuition in subjects such as geology and environmental sciences, where it is impossible to film footage of past events, or for medicine or nuclear science, where it would be dangerous and/or unethical to conduct 'live' experiments.

APP

The term 'app', an abbreviation of 'application', refers to a **software** programme that is designed to be used on a **web enabled** device, such as a **smartphone** or **tablet**, to perform a specific task or function. The term is also sometimes used to refer to larger, multi-function, end-user software programmes by computer manufacturers. Many apps can be **downloaded** free, while some need to be purchased from online app stores. There is a vast array of education-related apps freely available to support informal and formal learning or to assist in study-related activities for children, young people and adults. A few illustrative examples of areas of education in which apps are commonly used include: supporting school pupils in learning times-tables, to help college and university students capture and organise reference material, for communications, tracking health and fitness, and for learning new languages.

ARTIFICIAL INTELLIGENCE

The ability of a computer system to perform tasks normally associated with a human, such as complicated decision-making, reasoning, and robotics.

ASSESSMENT

A general term for the process used to give a value to a learner's knowledge and/or progress in attaining relevant skills. We can broadly classify assessments into two types: *formative*, through which learners can test their understanding of a subject before moving on to other stages; and *summative* assessments, which will count towards the overall grade or mark obtained by a learner for a particular piece of work. Normally a formative assessment does not count towards a final grade, but rather it gives learners an indication of their progress and level of attainment to allow them to fully form their ideas. Formative assessments may be designated as self-assessment exercises that remain with the learner, or the learner can be required to submit the work to a tutor or perhaps to a **discussion board**, where it is open to scrutiny by the class. Good practice dictates that assessments should be related to predefined learning outcomes for a **module** or a particular piece of work. Increasingly, it is common that assessments will also be linked to a pre-agreed marking strategy to enable an audit of the allocation of marks, and this may be shown to learners in advance of attempting the assessment in order to indicate areas of importance.

Due to some of the initial concerns relating to elearning, such as 'How do we know that the person being assessed is actually doing the assessment?' it is significant that the standards and controls on elearning assessment have pushed the barriers towards good practice for educational assessments in general. The difficulties of working remotely and with **asynchronous** access have forced tutors and teachers to be very clear in their instructions to **online** learners, and to indicate precisely the location of resources, methods of study and expectations of standards. A further concern is that the technology should not become a barrier to learning and should in fact provide additional resources for learners.

It is natural that progressive attempts to develop **open learning**, and to provide educational resources that allow for more **flexible learning**, have included a structured re-thinking of assessment techniques to ensure that each assessment actually tests what its designers think that it is testing. This would include a mix of assessment types that allows learners to capitalise on their strengths and address their weaknesses (e.g. a learner who has difficulty in presenting a clear written explanation may perform better at a verbal assessment). One solution that has been adopted widely in order to work with, rather than against, the technology has been the design of **blended learning** solutions in order to fit different types of learning needs to a range of technologies and pedagogies. This has the additional advantage of creating a wide variety of different types of assessment, from straight essays or reports, to varieties of online presentation in the virtual learning environment (**VLE)** or by **videoconferencing**. Most forms of assessment focus on the individual performance of learners, and this can be automated **multiple-choice**-type tests in some forms of **CBT** or other forms of computer marked assessments (CMAs), as opposed to tutor marked assessments (**TMAs**).

Some forms of assessment emphasise **groupwork** and/or team performance as important skills to acquire for later life, and marks are awarded for the level and quality of the role of each team member as well as for the result of the group process. More recently, there has been a recognition of the value of **interaction** online, both to give support to learners and to facilitate **peer-to-peer** learning exchanges. This in turn has resulted in some online courses allocating a proportion of the marks towards learners' overall grade to reflect the quality, regularity and consistency of their online contribution, e.g. the messages **posted** on a module discussion board as part of a structured dialogue between tutors and learners. A further development has been the recognition by some course designers that learners can compile an **eportfolio** containing a variety of different types of assessment in order to truly reflect the skills/abilities of the learner. As in so many other aspects of education, care needs to be taken not to over-assess the learner as this often results in a shallow form of learning in order to pass specific aspects of the course rather than a deeper comprehension of information-gathering, problem-solving and critical analysis.

Finally, there is almost universal agreement that the value of all types of assessment is significantly enhanced by the quality and speed of **feedback** given to learners on their work.

ASYNCHRONOUS LEARNING

The term is used to describe the use of the **internet** for access to a learning environment at times and locations to suit the user. It is most commonly applied to **online** discussion groups in which messages from students and from **tutoring** build up over an extended period. The primary advantage is flexibility in being able to fit learning around other commitments, but a major educational outcome is the time for reflection between **postings** and the opportunity to refine messages before posting. It has been likened to an extended seminar in which students learn from each other with the guidance of the tutor. Asynchronous learning can be contrasted with **interactivity** that is **synchronous**.

ATTACHMENT

This is usually a larger piece of writing, an image, or some other form of electronic file that is sent along with a shorter, explanatory **email** message. A common use is where a computer file containing some piece of reference material needs to be sent to several members of a group. The attachment could, of course, be sent as a **post** to online **communities** or a course **discussion board**, but it could also simply be sent attached to a short email to two or three relevant people. While text might be sent by cutting-and-pasting into the body of an email message, using an attachment has the advantage of retaining the original format and style, as well as appearing tidier to the reader. It is common for images, maps and similar content to be sent as **JPEG** or **GIF** or **PDF** attachments that would be difficult to include within the body of an email text. It is of course necessary that the recipient of the attachment has the same **software** that the sender used in order to ensure the **accessibility** of the attached file and allow it to be viewed.

AUDIO/VIDEO CLIPS

These are short files containing sound and/or video images that can be sent between users, either as an **attachment** to an **email** or by means of a **hyperlink** connecting it to a relevant **webpage**. Sound and video clips are frequently used in elearning as a way to add richness to the learning experience, rather than just using text to encourage the **motivation** of the learner, and to provide an additional element of **interaction** between the tutor and the learner in a remote location. Simple examples might include an audio/video clip that is placed on the **VLE** and accompanies a PowerPoint presentation on a certain topic. The learner can step through the PowerPoint slides to the accompaniment of the voice of the tutor talking through the presentation and explaining key points. Video clips not only provide the semblance of some social contact for learners (in contrast with textual **emoticons**) but also offer opportunities to demonstrate moving objects, such as engine parts, or chemistry experiments in a controlled environment. Their use in learning activities has been somewhat restricted until recently due to the fact that both image and sound files can require a very large memory allocation for any substantial piece of recording and, consequently, cause problems for users attempting to **download** and run any of these clips on a home computer. The increasing popularity and availability of **broadband** links to the **internet** is likely to overcome this difficulty for some users, although users with narrower **bandwidth** may continue to make use of learning centres. The need to be inclusive of students with varying levels of **ICT** access means that the **course design** of online learning resources will still require careful consideration as to when and how audio and video clips are incorporated in course resources.

AUDIOCONFERENCE

A form of many-to-many communication that utilises the telephone as a communication medium, used both for **tutoring** students in discussion as well as for **peer-to-peer** collaboration. Unlike a **videoconference**, it uses a relatively simple form of technology that most people are comfortable using in everyday life, though of course it lacks the visual impact of the videoconference. The basic method is for the tutor (or chairperson) to arrange a mutually convenient time to link all the participants together on a synchronous telephone call, working to a pre-circulated agenda or discussion topic. Depending on the telecom provider used, participants either dial into a particular conference-code number or are dialled in automatically ahead of the pre-arranged time by the operator. Like videoconferences, **discussion boards** and other methods of remote conferencing, the use of audioconference facilities requires a certain level of self-discipline and etiquette for the conduct of meetings.

Due to the fact that participants are not able to see body language or other visual clues, the chairperson, or **moderator**, needs to repeatedly check that other participants are a) still connected and b) understanding the content of the discussions. Simply asking a question such as, 'Does everybody understand/agree?' is more likely to cause confusion as participants, not knowing if the question is directed to themselves, are likely either to remain silent or all speak at the same time. For this reason, it is necessary to be specific in targeting questions and comments, and exercise the usual vigilance needed to discourage over-dominant speakers and encourage participation from quieter members of the meeting.

There is a long history of the use of audioconference facilities in the delivery of distance learning and as a means of engaging with students who are relatively remote (in geography and/or time) from their tutor, and the technique is commonly used well in combination with other learning resources in what is now being described as **blended learning**, or as one particular tool in the design of **distributed education**. The method has quite a high level of flexibility for delivering support to students who are learning from sites other than a central campus. For example, a tutor can conduct a discussion on a particular theme with two students or twenty (usually around twelve participants, for no longer than half an hour at a time, is ideal); participants can be contacted at home, at work, or even on the move; conferences can be at any mutually convenient time or day; and calls can be recorded or used in (**synchronous** or **asynchronous**) combination with other learning resources, such as printed materials, workbooks, **webpages**, or learning resources on an **MLE**, to produce a very rich learning experience. Audioconferencing may experience something of a renaissance as it becomes easier to phone directly from the user's computer, using applications such as **Skype** or other voice-over-internet forms of **software**, and to combine this with a **VLE**, on-screen presentations, video **graphics** or other **animations**.

AUGMENTED REALITY

A technique of imaging which superimposes digital data over a real environment in real time to create a new, enhanced environment, which integrates the two sources of information. Examples might include the addition of digital labels to identify parts in mechanical or medical operations. Distinct from **virtual reality**, which uses digital information to create artificial environments.

AUTHENTICATION

The process by which a computer system attempts to verify that a user is entitled to access a computer or a **network**, usually by a unique combination of user identification, **password** and **internet service provider (ISP)** address when a user **logs on** to a computer. The authentication process gives the appropriate users access through the network **firewall** to an environment of **trust** (such as a **VLE, MLE** or other online **community**) and is designed to ensure that only approved users get access to secure areas of the network.

AVATAR

Derived from a Hindu concept, in computing terms an avatar is a virtual representation of a human body. Its use is mainly confined to on-screen representation of the players in online **gamification**, who can be manipulated by instructions from the players and thus interact with other players via *their* avatars. In general terms, it is any virtual representation of a sentient being in an **online** environment, and could include humans or animals in other forms of online interactive media such as telepresence meetings and/or some forms of interactive **videoconferencing**.

BANDWIDTH

A measure of the amount of information that can flow through an information channel communicating data between computers. Bandwidth is commonly measured in bits of information per second, with higher-bandwidth facilities (**broadband**) allowing transmission of a greater volume of data, with greater speed and accuracy. A **modem** connection to an internet **server** is a typical example of a low-bandwidth connection; an Ethernet connection within a **local area network** is an example of a high-bandwidth connection. Higher-bandwidth transmissions allow a greater versatility in the design of **courseware**, enabling design teams to incorporate not simply large, complex files, such as book chapters or reports, but also **audio/video clips** and graphical **animations**. The combination of text, sound and moving images can be used to demonstrate practical learning activities such as laboratory experiments, moving engine parts or simulated field trips. Care needs to be taken when designing course materials for high-bandwidth users because, though the effects can be stunning and produce a rich learning environment, the inability of low-bandwidth users to **download** or view the resources frequently results in frustration and a consequent lack of student **retention**. Low-bandwidth connections commonly result in long delays in transmitting and receiving information, particularly large files and **webpages**.

BEHAVIOURISM

Behaviourism is a branch of educational theory and research which was the dominant school of thought in the period from the 1920s to around the early 1960s, and which sought to understand human and animal learning in relation to stimulus-and-response interactions and positively and negatively reinforced behaviour. Behaviourism and behaviourist learning theories are predominantly concerned with arranging the external environment to support the conditions for learning as 'observable' changes in behaviour, and they considered the mind (which could not be observed) as unknowable. While many of the educational principles and practices associated with behaviourism were subsequently challenged by **cognitivism** and subsequently **constructivism**, the focus on arranging the learning environment to create the optimum conditions for learning to occur remains a key concern within contemporary **instructional design** and **learning design** approaches, theories and models. Behaviourist approaches can also be identified in practices that include, for example, the selective release of course materials or feedback based on successful completion of self-tests in the **VLE**.

BIT/BYTE

In computing, a byte is a collection of eight bits, each bit being a single piece of digital information (i.e. a 1 or a 0 denoting on or off). The only context where elearners are likely to encounter the term with any relevance is in relation to descriptions of large files that are sent as **attachments** to **emails** or messages to a **discussion board**. For example, a kilobit (Kb) is one thousand bits, a Megabit (Mb) is one million bits, and a Gigabit (Gb) is one thousand million bits.

BITE-SIZED LEARNING

In relation to digital education, 'bite-sized learning' is a term that is increasingly in use to refer to small, focused episodes of learning activity supported by digital **online** educational content (for example, audio or video material, **podcasts**, interactivities) or engagement in time-limited online tasks. One common example of this is the use of language learning **apps** to support the learning of a few new words or a common phrase each day.

Bite-sized learning can also be used in formal educational contexts; for example, a student watching a short video or **animation** of a practical activity, lab procedure, or other specific task before then carrying out that task. Bite-sized online learning, sometimes referred to as micro-learning, and it has also been extended into the area of continued professional development (CPD) for practitioners as a means for new knowledge and skills to be acquired flexibly around other daily commitments. Many universities, for example, now offer bite-sized online CPD opportunities through which lecturers can devote a short amount of time each day, or at a few points over a week, to learn how to use particular digital technologies or digitally enabled approaches that they can then use to support their own students.

BLENDED LEARNING

The term 'blended learning' became popular around the year 2000 and is now widely used in North America, the UK and Australia, and in academic as well as training circles. The original and still most common meaning refers to combinations of **online** and **face-to-face** (**f2f**) teaching. However, other combinations of technologies, locations or pedagogical approaches are increasingly being identified as examples of blended learning. For example:

- Where both **synchronous** and **asynchronous** technologies are used on an online course;
- Where combinations of formal and informal learning are used in workplace professional development;
- Where students are accessing course material and resources from a variety of locations – home, learning centre, college, etc;
- Where technology is used to redesign high-enrolment courses to enhance quality and reduce costs.

In reality, any course or even any learning experience almost inevitably involves a combination of different inputs: reading, thinking, writing, **tutoring** and talking to peers. Consequently, as the use of the term widens, it becomes less and less useful as a descriptor. Critics have come to the fore to claim that 'blended learning' is simply a new label that is being applied to old goods, but, although this may be true, it neglects to consider two important elements. First, in historical terms, online learning is a new mode of learning opportunity, and it has the potential to fundamentally alter the relationship between the learner and the tutor. How this blend is able to mature and combine the best aspects of both 'conventional' and online media is as yet an unfinished chapter. It is therefore rather early to dismiss experimental combinations of different learning blends that incorporate new technology as simply a marketing gimmick. Second, even if 'blended learning' is simply a new label on a method of education that tutors have been practicing for several decades, the fact that it has now been recognised as a legitimate, even desirable, approach to educational resource delivery has profound implications for the ways in which we embark upon course construction.

Blended learning is said to combine the power and effectiveness of the classroom with the flexibility and anytime nature of elearning and allows learning to be more tailored and more individualistic, while at the same time allowing greater reach and distributed delivery. Without getting into the eternal debate of 'teaching versus learning', the strong implications of the term 'blended learning' are that:

- diverse opportunities to present learning resources and tutor-student and student-student communications are more flexible and more desirable than narrower, one-track solutions;
- individual learners will, if encouraged to play an active part in their own educational development, select learning resources from different media and sources that are more convenient and appropriate for their personal situations. This might include the alternative option (or replacement) of lectures with **webcasts** or recorded CDs, of live discussions with asynchronous online discussion, of targeted, **digitized** articles in the absence of a nearby university library with thousands of books, or the provision of structured reading lists that link to online academic journals.

The questions that are repeatedly asked about blended learning centre around: What is the best blend? Is one blend more effective than another? So far, there is little evidence from which to generalise, but many educators and trainers seem to conclude that the answers lie in a cultural shift away from teaching and training and towards learning and the **motivation** of learners. A significant preoccupation for course designers and educational analysts is how to intentionally design the optimum blended learning course, rather than allow historical circumstance, chance and individual tutor biases to dictate the mixture of the final blend. This approach stresses diversity in the development of learning materials, **courseware, assessments** and supporting resources, and is becoming synonymous with **distributed education**, although the latter also has strong geographical implications.

An alternative though much less common term is 'hybrid learning'. Figure 1 shows a schematic description of blended learning.

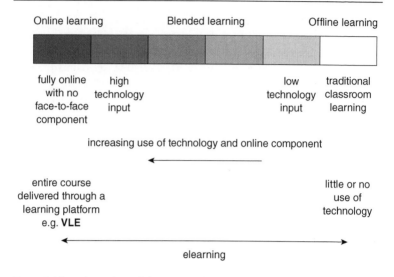

Figure 1 The relationship of elearning to distributed learning

Source: An introduction to elearning: Using the NLN materials within a Virtual Learning Environment (Adapted by Fiona Rennie)

BLOGGING (WEBLOGGING)

A weblog, web log, or simply a blog, is a **web** application which contains periodic time-stamped **posts** on a common **webpage.** These posts are often but not necessarily in reverse chronological order. Blogs are usually written by a single author, rather like a diary, but occasionally they are group activities with many authors. Most weblogs enable visitors to leave public comments, which can lead to a community of readers centred around the blog; others are non-interactive.

A blog is and has always been more than the **online** equivalent of a personal journal. The blog adds to the form of the diary by incorporating the best features of **hypertext**: the capacity to link to new and useful resources. But a blog is also characterised by its use of a personal style, and this style may be reflected in either the writing or the selection of links passed along to readers. Blogs are, in their purest form, the core of what has come to be called personal publishing. What makes blogs so attractive, in both the educational community and the **internet** at large, is their ease of use. A blog owner can edit or update a new entry without worrying about page formats or **HTML** syntax.

Educators are still in the experimental phase of understanding the value of this medium. There is little doubt that as an educational process, regular blogging develops a range of skills such as: **digital literacy**, critical thinking, writing and self-expression skills. What is more significant is that it offers students a chance to reflect on what they are writing and thinking, and to do this over a sustained period of time. If comments by other students are encouraged, the student is writing for an audience of peers and can learn the art of engaging readers in a sustained conversation.

However, when blogging is used by teachers in a prescriptive way, such as, 'Write a blog on the subject of XXX', the value of blogging is very much constrained and it becomes another writing exercise. As many writers have noted, blogging is, at its best, a conversation and needs a purpose and an audience, but not prescribed topics.

Blogging **software** breaks down into two major categories: hosting services and installed applications. A hosting service is a **website** that will give you access to everything you need in order to create a blog. It will offer a form for you to input your entries, some tools that allow you to create a template for your blog, and access to some built-in accessories. A remotely installed application is a piece of software that you obtain from the provider and install on your own website. These systems are similar to web-based applications such as ColdFusion or Hypermail. Because of this, the number of users is much lower, but those who do use them tend (arguably) to be more dedicated and more knowledgeable than those who use hosting services. Installed applications are also more suitable for institutional use since access can be controlled.

Some educators choose to use specific weblog software instead of traditional course management tools, such as the **VLE**, due to the closed nature of the latter. These educators may prefer that their course content be openly available and shareable with colleagues. They may also want discussions or student work to be carried over and available after a specific course ends. Weblogs are not closed environments and allow content to remain after a course ends. It is also possible to use weblog content within the **VLE**. This provides many interesting options for educators, including adding dynamic content to a course and sharing content across multiple courses within a degree programme.

Blogging is also a useful tool for teachers. They can use it to build an archive of readings and research resources. They can share their reflections on research or **pedagogy** with colleagues, and use it for instant publishing of ideas, innovations or other results.

In organisations, blogging is being used as a knowledge management tool. It works well as a way of disseminating tacit rather than explicit information. In this regard, some commentators note the similarities that blogging shares with storytelling. Stories convey understanding because they are told in context. Context conveys emotions, triggers individual and group memories, and provides intuition and insights to events. Bloggers establish context over an extended period of time, and, since their audience is usually made of regular visitors, context can be implied or can be explicitly **hyperlinked** to a previous entry.

Despite these indications, there is general agreement that trying to define precisely what blogging is actually about is an exercise in futility because blogs are constantly shifting, evolving and becoming something else.

Those who have been involved in elearning since the beginning will notice a similarity between these comments about blogging and earlier promotions of **computer conferencing**, and before that, of **email**. Similar learning benefits are common to all: **interaction**, communication, reflection, wide audience, opportunity for **feedback** and refining ideas, archiving and re-reading possibilities, and so on. What makes blogging better or different than computer conferencing? Students who have used both say that blogging is more personal and sustained, that it offers a better opportunity to build expertise, and in the end that it is more fun!

BLUETOOTH

This is a type of wireless radio communications standard that enables secure, low-cost signals to be exchanged between devices such as personal computers, mobile phones, **laptops** and personal digital assistants (PDAs). The standard is ideal for mobile users who need to communicate with a **network** to exchange information. It is designed to be used with devices which have low power consumption, and will allow the devices to exchange information automatically when they come within range (usually a few tens of metres) They are ideal for **wireless networks** and have been used, for example, within small confined areas such as an open-plan office to communicate between the mouse and the computer, or the computer and a printer.

BRAINSTORMING

Brainstorming is a method of generating ideas amongst a group of learners. It works well in an elearning context as students can add ideas over time. The two key elements are: defining the problem or idea and establishing an environment in which anything related to the topic can be contributed without criticism or rejection. It can operate either formally or informally with a large or small group.

BRING YOUR OWN DEVICE

With the decrease in the cost of computers and the growth of **mobile learning**, there is a recognition that many learners prefer to use their own **laptops**, tablets and **smartphones**, rather than use the computers made available by their institution. As a result, some learning institutions are disinvesting in computer resource rooms in favour of more accessible working spaces and easy-access **wi-fi**.

BROADBAND

Broadband is the method of sending and receiving data over high-speed **networks**. It is most commonly associated with a far faster way of connecting a computer to the **internet** than is possible through a conventional dial-up method, which uses standard telephone networks. Broadband connections that use cable or asymmetric digital subscriber line (ADSL) have greater capacity to send data than those using standard telephone networks. This means that far more information can be transmitted in the same period of time than with a conventional dial-up connection – allowing faster viewing of **webpages**, faster **downloading** of files and faster access to **email**.

Broadband-supported learning offers a means to facilitate the introduction of innovative approaches to teaching and learning that privilege collaboration, shared knowledge construction, peer-to-peer **interaction** and **mentoring** unrestricted by geographic, cultural or temporal barriers.

Broadband is fundamentally changing the way research is conducted in the higher education sector. Researchers rely heavily on the internet to access research information and online journals, and to communicate with colleagues overseas. There is growing use of modelling and data visualisation in research to better understand complex processes, especially in fields such as environmental science and biotechnology. Such research is dependent on the availability of high performance computing and advanced networks to facilitate the manipulation and exchange of very large data sets. Those universities that lack sufficient **bandwidth** will increasingly find that they are unable to participate in key fields of research.

Newer technologies like wireless, mobile and broadband will increase immeasurably the possible blends for both campus-based and distance education. Mobile devices, such as personal digital assistants (PDAs), mobile phones, wireless **laptops** and tablet PCs, are being introduced into courses to increase flexibility, widen participation, allow more natural interaction and collaboration, and to use handwriting rather than keyboarding. Broadband, or high-speed internet access, brings a number of advantages to the education sector: speed, 'always-on' convenience and **multimedia** communication. At its simplest, high-speed internet access will allow the sort of fast response download and rapid **peer-to-peer** interaction that campus-based users in universities and corporate business have been used to for some time. Broadband is already blurring the divide between **face-to-face** (**f2f**) and online students, the more so as campus-based courses increasingly incorporate levels of online interaction in their learning plans.

BROWSER

'Browser' is a shorthand term for a '**web** browser'. This is a **software** application that allows users to access and interact with a **search engine** that is hosted on a **server** in order to view **webpages** that are written in **HTML**. Browsers that are currently popular include Internet Explorer, Firefox, Google Chrome, and Netscape.

CASE STUDY

The case study method has a long tradition in the teaching of law, business and medicine. Recently, its use has spread to other areas of the curriculum and particularly to an elearning context. Case studies are often used to demonstrate effective practice and to illustrate general principles through specific examples. In the UK, Jisc, the Joint Information Systems Committee, has devised a template to collect, document and disseminate case studies across the UK higher education community.

Figure 2 was developed by Jisc as part of the Pedagogy Strand of the Jisc eLearning Programme. More information is available at www.jisc.ac.uk /elearning_pedagogy.html for the strand and for case studies at www .jisc.ac.uk/search/case%20studies on the case studies developed as part of the Effective Practice with eLearning guide.

CHATROOM/CHATBOX

A simple form of computer-mediated communication (CMC) that allows users to participate in **synchronous** communication with each other, usually in the form of short **text messages**. The synchronicity distinguishes it from a **discussion board**, which is usually **asynchronous**. Most chatrooms are dedicated to particular themes or topics of common interest, and in this respect they could be considered small, temporary **communities** that are **online**. Some chatrooms may allow the users to represent themselves with an **avatar**, but they are mostly restricted to simple text communications, and users are required to include **emoticons** in order to convey emotions such as anger or humour. The limitations of the demands for synchronous access and the superficiality of many of the chatrooms have limited their potential for elearning, but they are still popular amongst teenagers and certain elements of the games and gaming community. Concern over opportunities for child abuse has led to a **password** protection system on most school chatroom facilities, but in this manner they can offer a fun and safe way to introduce children to the world of online communications.

Case study title	
Institution name	
Background [Give brief details of institution, type of learners and learning environment in which the activity/ies took place]	
Intended outcome(s) [Describe the objective(s) behind the practice outlined here]	
The challenge [Identity the issues that required attention or which prompted you to re-assess your previous practice]	
Established practice [Identify features of the practice previously in use - this may include any aspects which were subsequently amended]	
The e-learning advantage [Describe the benefits of the addition or amendment of an element of e-learning, as experienced by learners, practitioners and/or the institution as a whole]	
Key points for effective practice [Briefly identify the most important points in the case study for other practitioners - these may include risks as well as benefits]	
Conclusions and recommendations [A summary of how and why the practice outlined here has been effective]	
Additional information [Use this optional section to add related materials or content e.g. a lesson plan or a set of data, or to supply your email address]	

Figure 2 Template for case studies descriptions

CLIENT

This is a computer system that is able to access a remote service on another computer via computer **networks** that are connected by the **internet**. Common examples are the client **software** that we use to retrieve our **email** from the memory of the **server** that our **ISP** operates for us, or the client **browser** that we use to access and read **webpages**. It is becoming common practice that when new elearners begin a course they will be sent appropriate client software by their educational establishment to **upload** to their home/work computer to enable the learner to access educational resources and communications tools to aid their studies.

CLOUD COMPUTING

A form of computer **network** use that uses the **internet** to store and access information such as files, **software** and **apps**, as and when required, rather than hosting them on a personal computer or local server. In addition to the networking advantages, such as regular updating of resources, cloud computing allows access to a massive data resource, which is greater than could be contained on most personal devices. Cloud storage also enables access from distributed locations and mobile devices.

COGNITIVISM

Cognitivism is a branch of educational theory and research which came to dominance in the 1960s through to the late 1980s, and which is concerned with the nature of the mind, memory and how perception, cognition and intellectual development occur. This was a markedly different focus to that of **behaviourism**, which was predominantly concerned with the external environment and observable behaviour. Key concepts and concerns in cognitivism include cognitive dissonance (and bridging the gap between current knowledge and new knowledge that needs to be developed), semantic and visual memory, the organisation of knowledge in schemas, recall and reasoning, problem-solving and individual differences in learners.

Many of the ideas and proposals associated with cognitivism have influenced thinking and practice in relation to learning with or through educational technologies. This included a focus in the 1990s on different ways of structuring **hypertext**-based course materials to support **problem-based learning** or to encourage the development of rich, non-linear knowledge. Cognitivist educational research has led us to understand the benefits of aiding comprehension and recall by presenting complimentary verbal (text-based, audio) and visual (images, **animations**, video) material concurrently. **Constructivism**, which has been the dominant branch of educational theory from the 1990s, accepts much of what cognitivist learning theory proposes about the nature of cognition and the nature of memory, but contextualised to the individual and social nature of knowledge construction.

COLLABORATIVE WORK/LEARNING

The practice of collaborative work or collaborative learning amongst **online** educators is widespread. It has spawned its own acronyms: CSCW or CSCL, which stand for Computer Supported Collaborative Work or Learning, respectively. The definition of the term as applied to elearning is: work jointly carried out on an activity or project to gain knowledge or skills. In some respects, online collaborative activities bring together the unique and most valued attributes of elearning:

- communication and **interaction** amongst peers;
- structured learning devised by the course designer(s);
- access to the resources of the **internet**;
- opportunity for students to develop team working skills;
- learning by doing;
- small-group activity.

The size of the group and the length of time allowed for the activity are issues that need to be tailored to the individual context. A typical example of a collaborative activity in a distributed higher education situation where the students do not meet would be:

a group of five to seven with two to three weeks to complete the activity. Examples of collaborative activities would include: an online debate; constructing a website on one of the course topics; or writing a joint review of the best websites on a relevant topic, or of some specified journal articles.

The way in which the group works has been the subject of some discussion in the elearning literature. In particular, collaborative work has been distinguished from cooperative work. Where the group decides to split the work according to existing skills and assemble the different parts at the end, this is cooperative work. The participants cooperate, but they take on the part of the task they can already do. In collaborative work, there is more negotiation, commenting and sharing. The learning comes from the process of interacting, reflecting and collaborating on how to do the task. In collaborative learning, students give and receive help from their peers, they exchange resources and information, and they challenge each other and jointly reflect on their progress. In short, collaborative activities develop team working skills amongst the group through focusing on a common goal. In this way, collaboration helps to overcome some of the ill effects of competition that is the mainstay of much formal education.

There are a number of barriers to elearning through collaborative activities. First of all, it can be very time-consuming. Negotiating tasks in an **asynchronous**, distance learning environment can be difficult, especially when no one wants to assume the leadership role. One way of speeding up the process, at least in the early stage of the course, is for the tutor to assign roles. This reduces the experience of negotiation for students, but the aim would be for students to negotiate roles themselves in the next activity. The fact is that most students have more experience of competing with each other than with collaborating, so this skill needs to be developed over time.

A second problem is inherent with all forms of collaboration, whether online or offline: participants contributing unequally. This becomes particularly contentious if the collaborative activity is part of the **assessment** of the course. Some tutors give one mark to everyone in the group. Others have devised a system whereby students grade each other's work, sometimes including a self mark as well as a tutor mark. Yet another alternative is an assignment in which part of the work is collaboratively produced and the other part is individual (e.g. an introduction and summary written separately by each student). This means that the student receives an individual mark made up of the group collaborative mark plus the mark for the student's own work.

Collaborative activities require good design skills on the part of the tutor(s). Finding topics and collaborative processes that work well in a particular discipline needs practice and experimentation. Equally critical to the success of collaborative working is the quality of **tutoring**: knowing when to intervene and how much to contribute are again skills that are only acquired through experience. Some tutors start off the activity and do not intervene at all until the end, when they perhaps provide a summary or overview of the collaborative process. Others keep a close watch on the interactions and are ready to intervene if they think the collaboration is floundering. They might **email** individual students to suggest a way forward or a contribution they might make. Or they might add comments to the collaboration space to try to model how the students might interact. Occasionally, tutors will invite or assign students to take on the tutor's role in order to develop leadership skills in the group.

Another difficulty with online collaboration, compared with **face-to-face (f2f)** collaboration, is the reticence students feel about contradicting or challenging each other to explain what they mean. This is undoubtedly due to the lack of visual clues in the online environment, and as students become more comfortable interacting online, they tend to become more assertive. Nevertheless, the tutor needs to encourage students to challenge ideas through modelling this process in response to students' messages.

Online collaborative work usually takes place through asynchronous discussion. However, it is possible and can be beneficial to include some **synchronous** discussions. Technologies for synchronous interaction include: text chat, shared screen plus text chat, and full **audioconference** and **videoconference**. Synchronous interaction provides immediate **feedback**, so it can help with negotiations. Social processes are also important for successful collaboration, and a synchronous session can provide greater social presence than the asynchronous environment.

There is a range of websites or portals about collaborative learning. A particularly good one geared for higher education is an Australian resource (see https://sydney.edu.au/education_social_work/learning_teaching/ict/theory/collaborative_learning.shtml) that contains a large number of online articles, journals and books about collaborative learning, a series of guest editorials and a section on technologies to support online collaboration. A site for the school sector is the Global School-Net Foundation (http://www.globalschoolnet.org/), which has been operating since 1984 to link school children around the world for joint projects.

COMMUNITY OF INQUIRY

The concept of a community of inquiry as developed by Garrison et al. (2000) provides a framework for considering and facilitating the **collaborative work** of learners. It extends the learning theory of **constructivism** in building knowledge together and recognises the importance of the environment of the learner in shaping their learning experience. In addition to the **peer-to-peer** learning aspect, the concept emphasises the need to acknowledge social **presence**, both of the learner(s) and the tutor(s). The activity of the community can be harnessed to co-create meaning, explore methods of inquiry and confirm understanding. The idea of a community of inquiry is regarded as being especially relevant to online learning, with its ability to enable **networks** of learners to collaborate through **social media** and **activity-based learning** opportunities.

COMMUNITY OPEN ONLINE COURSE (COOC)

COOCs are open courses for adult learners, delivered via the COOCs open online environment and based on a widening access and **open education** ethos in which the COOCs **platform** 'provides a place where anyone can teach and learn anything for free' (Shukie, 2015). Founded by Peter Shukie, COOCs is also a non-profit community-focused organisation with participation in the activities of COOCs guided by the COOCs community code. As a model and approach to open online education that is focused on widening **accessibility** to adult education for those who may not necessarily have had prior tertiary educational experiences, COOCs has attracted considerable interest in the education sector.

COMMUNITIES

The term 'virtual communities' has increasingly been applied to communication **networks** in which the participants are not located in the same geographical place but are distributed across the globe.

Unfortunately, the term seems to have almost as many definitions and descriptions as the 'traditional' communities of place, and arguments still emerge as to what is and is not an **online** community. An online community is a social network that uses computer support as the basis of communication amongst members instead of **face-to-face (f2f)** interaction. Two crucial aspects in the development of interactive learning networks, whether online or on-site, are the swift establishment of **trust** between the participants and the development of **collaborative learning** activities. These collaborative activities may include small groups of students reading material on different topics and preparing summaries for the rest of the class, as well as debates, group projects, **role play** and collaborative essays, **case studies** or research plans.

A key feature to recognise is that, in the development of this type of interactive network, the community of learners becomes the learning network as much as the computer-based communications system that supports it. Critics of the social value of online communities maintain that online communication, such as **email**, creates the sensation of being part of a community of people, interacting for the common good, but is substantially an illusion. This is difficult to counter, for two main reasons. First, the complex and diverse interactions that take place in 'real' communities of place are not fully understood, and many are contested by academics (e.g. we appear to regard our regular network of telephone contacts, or our superficial but regular contacts made through our work, as real communities although we do not reside together). Second, the scope and depth of online contacts is so wide, from the occasional email inquiry from a friend-of-a-friend, to active many-to-many academic discussion lists, to the detailed collaborative information sharing on groove networks, or other shared work spaces, that it seems foolish and irresponsible to catalogue all online relationships as illusory or superficial. While it is true that electronic communications (phone, **videoconferences**, email and shared **desktops**) create the illusion of proximity between participants, the question is whether proximity is a mandatory requirement for a community, or whether, in this instance, the liberating results of technology have allowed us to mitigate, if not remove, the tyranny of distance.

Though most early sociological work related to the concept of community as a physical territory where residents interact, there was also a contrasting view of community as an interactional field held together by the human need to interact with other human beings. The

internet can be used to create abstract places (virtual offices, **online libraries**, online work spaces and spaces for **peer-to-peer** interactive **gamification**), representations of the self (online identities) and abstract interactions (with other identities and with automated tasks), but it is this latter view of community which has come to be applied to online social networks.

At the very least, a community seems to be distinguished by a shared understanding of its boundaries, whether these are geographical or defined by particular areas of common interest. Common activities help to create a sense of community by providing a common sense of identity with which the members of the community can associate themselves. It may be useful to think of community as both the outcome and the context of informal networking, with the 'well-connected community' being achieved when people feel part of a web of diverse and interlocking relationships.

In both communities of place and online communities, it is important to understand that networking is a vital component of community development practice because it creates the conditions for robust, yet flexible, forms of collective action. A key community-building element resulting from social networking is the fostering of **trust** between the members of the network. Through the sheer number and speed of possible connections, the **web** has emerged as a powerful new technological vehicle for harvesting the personal experiences of others, and the construction of tools that attempt to make this collective activity more visible (and accessible) is a major research field. The fact that these connections can be somewhat distant, impersonal and even largely anonymous (the user shares only what s/he wants to share) can be a strength as well as an obstacle to elearning.

Simply because an online community has a less tangible physical presence (because the community is dispersed and may never meet face-to-face), this does not negate its existence. A useful comparison might be made with our references to the political 'sphere of influence', in which subtle civic and political communications and allegiances may operate without a face-to-face network of players. Similarly, the social construction made by economists called 'the market' to describe the local or global interplay of economic processes involving supply and demand is not weakened because there is no physical market-place where all the participants can sit down face-to-face to negotiate their complex deals. The use of the 'virtual community' as a term to describe computer networked interactions is not consistent if it is not also applied to earlier forms of distributed interactive networks. It was a useful term to give a shorthand description of the exciting and rapid appearance of a wider range of global connections through CMCs, but on closer analysis, with more persistent usage, the term has become an over-used, redundant and misleading appellation.

This sense of community is derived from the participants' perception of being linked into a complex system of relationships and interaction, and these shared experiences help to foster group solidarity and a sense of common purpose. Online communities have been roughly classified into five different types:

1. Communities of purpose, formed by people who are trying to achieve a similar objective, who assist each other by sharing experiences, information and peer-to-peer knowledge.
2. Communities of practice, formed by groups of people sharing a similar profession or vocation who seek to share experiences and facilitate professional exchange (which may also add value to offline networks).
3. Communities of circumstance, which are similar to communities of practice but are generally more personally focused, or related to life experiences, and not driven by professional activities.
4. Communities of interest, linking people who share their ideas, passion and knowledge in a common interest or theme, but who might know very little about each other outside this shared interest.
5. Communities of users, who are represented by the more innovative and interactive business networks that allow customer-to-customer exchanges, including the sharing of information, reviews and specific themed discussions.

In an increasingly electronically networked world, we may occupy more than one of these communities at different times of our day, working, learning and socialising. Online groups have the ability to connect with their community of interest at any time of day or night to share information or solicit help, and it is common that online relationships also move to include other forms of communication, e.g. telephone, post and/or face-to-face interaction.

We can list three key criteria that define successful online communities:

1. Self-generated evolution, where members of the community generate the content for the site and take decisions to influence its growth, adaptation and evolution.

2. Involvement and interactivity, through which members participate and interact with other members of the community (e.g. through email, **discussion boards** or **synchronous** chat).

3. Frequent and short visits that encourage members to come back to the site repeatedly in order to share their ideas with other community members as part of the process of establishing a collective identity and sense of trust between members of the community.

There is a clear indication that the participants in online communities are not attracted to them due to the provision of tools alone; they need to be able to recognise a common bond with other members of that community. It is this shared set of experiences which provides the potent stimulant of learning opportunities. According to this, the true function of a community is to provide an agreed regulation and discipline and a conduit for self-expression that is consistent with the greater good of the participant group as a whole. A key mechanism for achieving this is through fostering social institutions, which extends the concept of community beyond clusters of like-minded enthusiasts in common interest groups to networks of distinct but independent institutions. These heterogeneous networks differentiate the framework of a community from its constituent, narrower, common interest groups.

COMPUTER-BASED TRAINING (CBT)

'Computer-based training' is a term commonly used in corporate training circles, whereas 'computer-assisted instruction' (CAI) was the comparable term in education. With the advent of the **web**, both terms are passing out of use. CBT is usually a stand-alone package for training employees in company processes or in computer skills. Most packages contain tests, often **multiple choice questionnaires**, and the results may be logged so that the employee cannot progress without passing. The main limitation of CBT is that it is costly and time-consuming to produce, especially when **graphics** or **animations** are included. For large training requirements with a relatively unchanging subject matter, CBT may still be cost-effective. Many computers contain short CBT sequences for users to learn about the facilities they offer. The term 'computer-based learning' (CBL) is also sometimes used in elearning, especially for the provision of extra 'remedial' tutorials in difficult areas (e.g. maths or statistics).

COMPUTER CONFERENCING

The terms 'computer conferencing' and the similar 'computer-mediated communication' (CMC), are early names for what is now called elearning. As these terms pre-date the **web**, they largely concerned the communications side of **online** learning; **software**, which integrates online content and communication, only became prevalent with **VLEs**. Consequently, literature referring to computer conferencing focuses on the kind of software that facilitates textual **interactions** amongst students and the tutor, on the **asynchronous** nature of the communication and on the impact on the evolving conversation created by the opportunity for reflection. The novelty of this kind of interaction has largely ceased to be the focus of research, although many researchers continue to study the processes, the pedagogical value and the success of online communication.

The reasons for teachers introducing computer conferencing remain unchanged:

- students are distributed geographically;
- the demand for more flexible offerings;
- the perceived advantages of **blended learning**;
- the need for students to develop **ICT** skills.

The limitations of the medium for education are also fundamentally unchanged, although VLEs have increased the potential for more varied forms of communication (e.g. **synchronous** interaction, **video and audio clips, blogging** and **instant messaging**). Nevertheless, the experience of discussing academic issues through text is challenging to learners accustomed only to **face-to-face** (**f2f**) interaction. The lack of visual and physical presence is something that a minority of learners find hard to accept, and they never seem to regard textual communication as a vehicle for learning. Asynchronous online **interaction** can also be time-consuming, both for the tutor and the students. Busy students who have to fit their studying around employment, family and other responsibilities often find that online interaction is not an efficient use of their limited time. Moreover, computer conferencing does not demand their attention in the way that more immediate life situations do; consequently, logging on to the online discussion can easily be pushed to the bottom of their list of things to do. This leads to the feeling of guilt and frustration which many students of online courses report.

The way in which computer conferencing is integrated into the rest of the course is critical to its successful use. If the use is marginal, or perceived by students to be optional, the strategic learners will focus their efforts on the essential elements of the course and **log on** rarely or not at all. It is particularly difficult (though not impossible) to develop rich and pedagogically valuable discussions when students see each other regularly on campus. Structured activities and assessed online contributions are two possible solutions to successful blended learning.

Two issues, which today are accepted as part of the medium, preoccupied early researchers of computer conferencing:

1. The perceived equality of this means of communication has been compared with face-to-face seminars, where speakers have to wait their turn to speak. With computer conferencing, all students can input messages whenever they are ready. Furthermore, the lack of visual cues puts all participants on an equal footing, regardless of colour, disability, facial characteristics or accent. Although this is true in theory, in reality students who are more articulate, who have easy online access or who want to dominate discussions still can and do. Without careful intervention by the tutor, the shy, inarticulate and less confident students can be marginalised online just as they can be face-to-face. One phenomenon which has been noted many times, however, is that the tutor does not dominate discussion online to nearly the same extent as happens in face-to-face seminars. Other researchers have noted that some students who rarely speak in face-to-face discussions take a greater part in online discussions. So while the medium does not guarantee equality of participation, it usually improves on the interaction patterns of face-to-face seminars.

2. The fact that messages in computer conferencing software are archived means that there is a **database** of interactions. Students can refer back to messages and use extracts from them in their assignments, and the tutor can use the archive to write a summary of the discussion or to grade students' contributions. In general, the archive distinguishes asynchronous communication from face-to-face seminars by being available rather than ephemeral.

In the past, when computer conferencing was a new phenomenon, one of the techniques used to motivate students and add focus to the discussions was to invite a guest lecturer to tutor the course for a week or two. Of course, this guest expert could enter the conference from anywhere, read messages and add comments. Often the expert would begin with an opening statement or use an existing paper as a background resource to spark off the discussion. As elearning has become commonplace now, this practice is used much less frequently. The novelty of online interaction has worn off and most experts are too busy running their own courses.

Another practice which began at the outset of educational computer conferencing was the provision of a social conference, where students were free to discuss matters not related to the course. Initially the purpose was to prevent social interaction taking place in the academic discussion conferences. It soon became apparent, however, that these social spaces fulfilled a very necessary function in building community and **trust**. Through humour, chit-chat and exchanges about their personal lives, students get to know each other and develop an awareness of themselves as a group. Unlike the practice of guest lecturers, social conferences continue to be used on most online courses.

The use of **emoticons** or smileys developed very early in the history of computer conferencing, as a way of overcoming the lack of para-linguistic clues. Initially, conferencing software was command line and offered no facilities for any kind of typeface emphasis such as high-lighting or emboldening. Happy, surprised and sad faces were used to provide some of this missing emphasis.

The term 'computer conferencing' was used alongside '**videocon-ferencing**' and '**audioconferencing**' when all three were very distinct media. The advent of the web has led to the **convergence** of these means of communication, such that the term 'computer conferencing' is rarely used now.

CONNECTIVISM

Connectivism was first proposed as 'a learning theory for the digital age' by George Siemens, and it places an emphasis on the fluid nature of **networks**, and the nodes and connections which comprise them, in relation to learning and the production of knowledge.

Within connectivism:

> Learning is a process that occurs within nebulous environments of shifting core elements – not entirely under the control of the individual. Learning (defined as actionable knowledge) can reside outside of ourselves (within an organization or a database), is focused on connecting specialized information sets, and the connections that enable us to learn more are more important than our current state of knowing.
>
> (Siemens, 2005)

Siemens and other leading proponents of connectivism, including Stephen Downes, have pointed towards the limitations of established learning theories, including **behaviourism, cognitivism** and **constructivism**, in offering perspectives that are directly relevant and applicable to living and learning in a networked society. Key questions posed by Siemens (Siemens, 2005), and to which connectivism has sought to offer a response, include: 'how are learning theories impacted when knowledge is no longer acquired in the linear manner?'; 'what adjustments need to made with learning theories when technology performs many of the cognitive operations previously performed by learners (information storage and retrieval)?' and 'how can we continue to stay current in a rapidly evolving information ecology?'

In relation to the above, Siemens (Siemens, 2005) defines the following principles of connectivism:

- Learning and knowledge rests in diversity of opinions;
- Learning is a process of connecting specialised nodes or information sources;
- Learning may reside in non-human appliances;
- The capacity to know more is more critical than what is currently known;
- Nurturing and maintaining connections is needed to facilitate continual learning;
- The ability to see connections between fields, ideas and concepts is a core skill;
- Currency (accurate, up-to-date knowledge) is the intent of all connectivist learning activities;
- Decision-making is itself a learning process. Choosing what to learn and the meaning of incoming information is seen through the lens of a shifting reality. While there is a right answer now, it may be

wrong tomorrow due to alterations in the information climate affecting the decision.

In 2008, George Siemens and Stephen Downes delivered for the first time the open online course 'Connectivism and Connective Knowledge' to facilitate an exploration of connectivism and the principles of connectivist learning in practice. Over 2000 participants from across the globe engaged in the course, which was delivered through distributed content and **RSS** feeds and was subsequently recognised as the first **massive open online course (MOOC)**.

The extent to which connectivism actually presents a new theory of learning, as opposed to a valuable epistemological or pedagogical position relating to learning in the context of digital networks, is debated in the wider literature. Other perceived limitations of connectivism relate to areas including supporting reflective learning and practice, development of domain-specific core skills and knowledge, and **assessment**.

CONSTRUCTIVISM

Constructivism is a theory about learning which posits that learners construct knowledge for themselves. Each learner individually constructs meaning as he or she learns. Elearning is strongly associated with constructivism as both are learner-centred rather than teacher-centred. There are a number of general principles of learning that are derived from constructivism and that are well supported through elearning:

- Learning is an active process in which the learner engages with ideas and interacts with other learners in order to construct meaning;
- Reflection on learning is another key component of constructivist theory. Learning consists of both constructing meaning and constructing systems of meaning;
- Learning involves language and self-expression. The **online** environment supports this function;

- Learning is a social activity: our learning is intimately associated with our connection with other human beings – our teachers, our peers and our families, as well as casual acquaintances;
- Learning is contextual: we learn in relationship to what else we know, what we believe, our prejudices and our fears;
- One needs knowledge to learn: it is not possible to absorb new knowledge without having some structure developed from previous knowledge to build on. The more we know, the more we learn;
- Learning is not instantaneous: it takes time to learn. For significant learning, we need to revisit ideas, ponder them, try them out, play with them and use them.

CONTENT AGGREGATION

In simple terms, content aggregation involves the process of searching for digital content on the same topic(s) from a range of sources, which could include news items, **blog** articles and **social media** posts, and then collating or 'aggregating' them into a single space or artefact.

Although the process can be done manually – for example, a **Twitter** user quickly bringing together all the Twitter content shared under a specific **hashtag** – content aggregation is normally an automated process. Typically, the user would use a chosen 'content aggregator' **app** or tool, through which they subscribe to various feeds and also set parameters around key words, the kinds of content they are interested in and search frequency. The content aggregator then brings together the content that has been located, within the content aggregator itself, for viewing by the user or by publishing it as a specific output that the user can receive themselves or opt to share publicly (e.g. embedded directly onto a **webpage** or social media account, or circulated via **email** or **social media** as a digital newsletter or **discussion board**). There are many content aggregation apps and tools available, including Pinterest, Nuzzel, diigo and papr.li. Uses of content aggregation within education include enabling teachers and lecturers to automatically produce and circulate newsletters or digests on particular topics, and allowing learners to create their own aggregated collections or artefacts.

Both content aggregation and **content curation** are important aspects of the activities learners, educators and practitioners would engage in within the contexts of their own professional learning environments and professional learning networks.

CONTENT CURATION

The main distinction between **content aggregation** and content curation is that the latter involves the user in making at least some decisions about the importance of the content they want to share, and in customising and otherwise tailoring how the content is organised and presented. For example, this can be done through providing short summaries of the articles, **blog** posts and videos they have sourced and explaining why they may be of interest to the intended readership, or through providing their own original content alongside that sourced from elsewhere. Content curation can also involve the curator in manually searching for the best, the most interesting or niche content to share with their learners or peers, or making value judgements relating to the best content from information that has been automatically aggregated.

Many content aggregator **apps** also support content curation, through options to edit and tailor in the ways described above. Common uses of content curation in education include to create resource collections, for **social bookmarking**, to engage students in digital storytelling, and for compiling **eportfolios** or producing collaborative **groupwork** artefacts.

Both content aggregation and content curation are important aspects of the activities learners, educators and practitioners would engage in within the contexts of their own professional learning environments and professional learning networks.

CONVERGENCE

In the context of **information and communications technology (ICT)**, this term describes the inter-operability of different forms of applications and devices which allows them to communicate with one another. The growth of convergence has been made easier as analogue technologies (e.g. magnetic-tape cassettes) have been replaced by digital sources of information. Convergence basically allows one piece of equipment or **software** to communicate with another. Examples of convergence in terms of elearning include the ability to utilise digital television or hand-held devices such as certain mobile phones for **surfing** the **internet**. Another example would be to take a picture with a digital camera that can then be **uploaded** to a **laptop** computer and then sent by **email** to a colleague or course tutor. Increasing convergence has allowed learners to communicate with their institutional **VLE** by using whatever **ISP** they choose to send email, to use mobile phones for **text messaging** to a **module discussion board** or to stream **videoconferences** onto their own desktop PCs.

As **networks** of varied devices are created and enlarged by convergence, we see a trend towards learners being able to access learning resources from all sorts of different locations (pervasive learning) or while they are on the move (**mobile learning**). To be most successful, the users should be unaware of the technicalities of convergence so that they are able to concentrate on using the device of their choice to communicate with another person or device without being deterred by the technology. Greater convergence allows greater flexibility in pursuing opportunities for **distributed education**, and with the spread of **wireless networks** it has become possible to link communications devices over the internet in more flexible ways than can be allowed for with fixed cabling (e.g. working on the move or in ad hoc meetings).

COOKIE

A cookie is a small file that can be sent to a computer by a **server** when a connection is made over the **internet**. When the server is contacted (e.g. when **surfing** the **web** for a particular product) the server sends a small file to the hard disk on the user's computer. The next time that contact is made with this server, the cookie on the user's computer is read by the server, enabling it to recognise the user and greet them by name. The information collected by the cookie can be used to gather information on individual users, and to create a user profile that can help customise individual preferences. An example might be that when a user connects to Amazon on their usual computer, the website greets the user by name and is able to recommend particular books or music that s/he might like. This is based upon a complex **database** that has recorded the previous items that the user has purchased from them, the items that s/he has **browsed** and a comparison with the purchasing preferences of other users who have selected some of the same products. There is a considerable potential for this type of user profile creation amongst elearners, but restrictions of **copyright** and data protection laws currently limit its application.

COPYRIGHT

This is the complex set of legal rights that is used to control the manner in which an idea is expressed, and how the idea is replicated. Common examples include the restricted right to copy text or images from books, magazines, journals and other media. The intention of copyright is to allow the 'owner' of the idea (such as a story, an explanation or a piece of creative work) to benefit from the idea for a fixed period of time. In a digital age, copyright causes problems because it has become much easier to replicate text digitally, change it slightly and incorporate it into another piece of work.

Copying a piece of work without acknowledging the source with a full reference is termed **plagiarism**, and it can prove to be problematic to detect in an elearning environment. Although short quotations and descriptive paragraphs can normally be used freely, the replication of entire journal articles and books (e.g. on a **VLE**) is normally copyright restricted and requires the payment of royalties. Many educationalists have argued that copyright operates against the spirit of information being freely available on the **internet** for educational purposes and therefore that copyright is losing its value in the digital age. Attempts to circumvent the restrictions of copyright include the use of educational portals that give secure access (**password** protected) to collections of **online** journals and e-books, as well as **digitizing** selected key articles for a course (for which a copyright fee is paid) and making these electronically available to authorised learners.

COURSE DESIGN

The design of course materials for elearning is the most crucial, but also perhaps the most contested, aspect of **online** learning. On the one hand, critics have tended to dismiss elearning as a poor substitute for 'the real thing' (i.e. conventional, classroom-based education), with students simply being encouraged to search the **internet** for learning resources and with little or no **tutoring** input. The use of the word 'virtual' in **VLE** and '**virtual university**' is a legacy of this thinking. On the other hand, proponents of elearning have claimed that a well-structured course can provide more contact between tutor and student than many 'conventional' courses, and that the educational experience is better because that tutor contact is applied in the context of the individual learner. Both advocates and detractors agree that good course design for elearning is more than simply giving out lecture notes and further reading suggestions by **posting** them on the **web** (although this seems still to be the case in some conventional courses!).

Thinking carefully about course design for elearning is not very different from thinking about good course design in a more traditional format, except that there are more varied forms of communication between participants, and greater diversity of formats for learning resources. The initial starting point must be a careful consideration of what it is that the tutor wants the students to have learned by the end of the **module**. These learning outcomes are then matched with appropriate types of **assessment**; following this, the design team needs to identify and select relevant sections of supporting evidence, additional reading, definitions of concepts and explanatory information that can assist the learner to acquire the appropriate level of understanding in the subject. In elearning, or in **distributed education** more generally, decisions need to be taken at this stage to select the most appropriate media, technologies and learning resources to share the different educational components with the learners. This is critical if the **ICT** resources and other media are to support the learning process rather than becoming a dominating factor in themselves. Good elearning not only captures the benefits of the **asynchronous learning** opportunities that are created but also exploits the advantages of a diverse range of digital resources available over the internet, such as:

- **Discussion boards** and/or **chatroom** facilities to encourage dialogue with students;

- **Audio/video clips** to provide learning resources other than simple text;
- **Hyperlinks** to other sources of information such as useful **web-pages**, links to portals and/or **online libraries**;
- Activities to promote **interaction** between learners, and between learner and tutor (either individually or in **tutor groups**);
- Opportunities for assessment, including self-assessment through activities such as **multiple choice questionnaires**, or perhaps **gamification**, or the incorporation of **animations** and **simulations**;
- Opportunities for students to receive **feedback** on their work and progress.

Many studies show, especially in the early stages, that the quality of support for learners (online and offline) is highly important for a successful learning experience. Careful course design is not cheap in comparison to more traditional educational development (particularly as costs are front-loaded), but studies would indicate that it need not be any more expensive in the medium term and, in fact, because of the scalability, might prove to be more cost-effective in the long term. Neither is elearning less of a workload for staff, though human resources might be deployed differently, according to the learning needs of any particular course. In selecting the specific blend in course design, it is important to appreciate two key points:

1. The learning situation of the participants: for example, it would be inappropriate to use **videoconferencing** to students if all that is required is to talk to them, or if learners would find it difficult to access such expensive and specialised facilities; **audioconference** facilities might be preferable. Similarly, directing learners to online journals and **digitizing** journal articles for inclusion in the VLE may not be appropriate if elearners lack **bandwidth** (such as **broadband**) and therefore experience difficulties in their ability to **download** the articles. Perhaps the articles could be recorded on compact disc (CD) and posted to the students.
2. The learning style preference of the learners. We know from experience that people learn best by different means: some people prefer to huddle up with a book; others prefer direct action, and still others would choose talking, or video images, to assimilate new information. Obviously, there are limitations, both technical and financial, on the provision of the same information in multiple

formats, but experiments with **blended learning** and with dual mode institutions would seem to indicate considerable scope for the expansion of this style in the future. The choice of the selected media format should reflect the nature of the learning activity and the type(s) of learning resources that are to be made available to the learner. This may allow for various combinations of media for different learners and learning situations; for example, a PowerPoint style presentation on a VLE, with an accompanying **audio** file, may suit one group of learners, while others might prefer to receive the PowerPoint slides as an **attachment** to an **email**, with a follow-up telephone call or audioconference discussion.

Selecting a course design that provides **motivation** for the elearner to engage with the learning resources, while not allowing the ICT to dictate the terms of that engagement, is tricky but of fundamental importance. Ideally, the technology should fade into the background as learners become more confident in using the **hardware** and **software** applications. Allowing some level of **self-direction** over the pace and style of the way that each elearner wants to learn can be a liberating as well as a richly stimulating experience.

COURSEWARE

This is any type of instructional or educational course delivered via a **software** programme or over the **internet**.

CREATIVE COMMONS

A system for identifying (mainly digital) resources which can be freely and openly shared, subject to certain conditions, thereby increasing **accessibility**. Conditions might include requiring an acknowledgement of the resource creator, or a specification that the resource can be shared except for commercial profit. The Creative Commons are a form of **open access**, which has been developed as an alternative to the more restrictive rules of **copyright**, which frequently prevent the open sharing of digital resources. Items included in the global pool of Creative Commons are usually badged with the code 'CC' and a two-letter license, which denotes the level of freedom to share the item.

CYBERSPACE

This is a term invented to describe the concept of the space where participants can meet **online** to form **communities** on the **internet** to share information, exchange ideas and generally take part in online discussion (and in the case of elearning, to access course content and resources). The term has science fiction origins but is now commonly used to explain the notion of a 'virtual place' where online information can be archived and exchanges can take place between individuals. In elearning terms, learners occupy cyberspace when they exchange **email**, join a **chatroom** or other CMC and when they take part in learning conversations on **discussion boards** or other **MLEs**.

CYBERSTALKING

This is the use of the **internet** and other means of electronic and digital communication technologies to harass, intimidate or frighten an individual, group or organisation, including through slander, false allegations or accusations, and other unsolicited and unjust communications.

DATA SECURITY

Digital data can be copied very quickly, with a high level of accuracy, and information shared across any **network** will be open to various levels of user **accessibility**. This is important to recognise, because all information conveyed across the **internet** may be subject to data theft and exploitation. Secure systems commonly employ a user **password** to control access to information and may use different levels of data **encryption** to prevent data being read by unauthorised users. Data security requires that all data should be stored in a secure environment, but also that sensitive information, such as name, date of birth and address, should not be disclosed in a manner that allows the identification of individuals to unauthorised people. Data security measures include controlling who has access to data and systems, robust password protection, data and device encryption, organisational data security policies, regular backing up of data and **cloud** storage.

DATABASE

A type of **software** designed to store and retrieve data in an ordered manner. Most database programmes will allow users to search for key themes, re-order data and perhaps allow elementary analysis of the results (e.g. produce graphs or other forms of **graphics**). An advantage of the more complex databases is that they can record multiple characteristics of a sample population and can therefore enable cross-comparison between variables. Connections to **web**-based databases are increasingly being used by commercial retailers to customise the selection of products that they can recommend to potential customers, and this technology has powerful educational potential when linked to resources such as **online libraries** and educational portals.

DESKTOP

In computing terms, the desktop is usually the image of the computer screen when the user first switches the computer on, and before any **software** applications are started or any 'windows' are opened. The desktop is used as a metaphor to refer to an actual desk top where the user can place any files and/or documents that they want to display. Usually the desktop will display a small number of **icons** of the most frequently used documents, files, folders and software applications that are used on that computer.

DIGITAL BADGE

HASTAC (Humanities, Arts, Science and Technology Alliance and Collaboratory) defines a digital badge as a:

> validated indicator of accomplishment, skill, quality, or interest that can be earned in many learning environments. Open digital badging makes it easy for anyone to issue, earn, and display badges across the web – through an infrastructure that uses shared and open technical standards.
>
> *Source:* https://www.hastac.org/initiatives/digital-badges

Digital badges are a common form of **micro-credentialing** and are used in informal and formal education and training opportunities, from school through to continued professional learning, to enable individuals to evidence the accomplishment of particular tasks and development of specific skills. Digital badges are also commonly used in many **MOOCs** and other open **online** courses to encourage or incentivise engagement and completion of particular aspects of the course.

DIGITAL DIVIDE

A term used to describe the discrepancy between people who have access to and the resources to use new information and communication tools, such as the **internet**, and people who do not. The term also describes the discrepancy between those who have the skills, knowledge and abilities to use the technologies and those who do not. The digital divide can exist between those living in rural areas and those living in urban areas, between the educated and uneducated, between economic classes, and on a global scale between more and less industrially developed nations.

DIGITAL LITERACY

A term given to the ability to understand and navigate the world of digital media. The term is (probably deliberately) diffuse to encompass the diverse manifestations of digital information, from **surfing** the **internet** or engaging with **social media**, to evaluating a **webpage** or manipulating **open educational resources**. The ability to participate effectively in the digital world, and to use digital sources of information, is seen as a key educational skill for the future, both in education and in the workplace. Competence levels of digital literacy are associated with the concept of **digital natives and immigrants**.

DIGITAL NATIVES AND IMMIGRANTS

A concept and term defined by Mark Prensky (2001), in which it is proposed that some (particularly younger) people are inherently more comfortable and competent with using digital technologies than other (older) people. While superficially a plausible concept, and still in wide use, the concept is now a contested one and subsequent research has shown that there is often as much variation in ability within generations as there is between generations. Contrasts with the **digital visitors and residents** model of online engagement.

DIGITAL SCHOLARSHIP

Martin Weller offers an intentionally broad definition of a digital scholar as being 'someone who employs digital, networked and open approaches to demonstrate specialism in a field' (Weller, 2011, p. 4). This can encompass the harnessing and use of digital tools, resources and spaces, and also digital bodies of evidence and data, to facilitate and communicate research, inquiry, reflection and narrative within the disciplinary domain of the scholar. Digital scholarship can involve the informal sharing of scholarly activities and outputs; for example, through disseminating ideas in development or work in progress through **blogging**, and through other informal and formal means of **open publishing**, including opting to publish peer-reviewed academic research papers in open journals. Importantly though, as Weller (ibid) observes, 'a digital scholar need not be a recognised academic'. Early-career academics, professional practitioners, and other subject experts or specialists can benefit from sharing their work, and engaging with their peers and wider research and disciplinary networks, through digital scholarship and associated practices.

There is also an increasing appreciation of the educational benefits that engaging in digital scholarship activities can offer students. This might be expressed through undergraduates producing coursework in digital forms that may have a relevance to others beyond the university, or in supporting postgraduate research students to make connections into their wider **networks** and to share and engage in dialogue about their research within those networks.

DIGITAL UNIVERSITY

The term 'digital university' has become an increasingly common one in educational research and literature in recent years, although it is used in various ways that place different emphases on the role of digital technologies and practices in higher education.

Within the literature to date, some uses of the term relate primarily to the concept of the digital university with reference to increased technological efficiencies in university processes and procedures, including scalability of courses, increased 'market share' of the higher education sector and competitive advantage of universities. Other uses of the term 'digital university' are to be found in the context of universities as a place for the development of critical **digital literacies** and capabilities, and 'transformational' developments of educational practice and the curriculum. The term, and the concept, remain diffuse and indeterminate at the time of writing. The various ways in which the concept of the 'digital university' can be critiqued, under-stood and enacted are explored by Johnston et al. (2019), who offer a perspective on the 'digital university' which relates to the location and co-location of universities and curricula, and how digital tools, spaces and practices can be used to extend higher education as a public good within wider societal and political contexts.

DIGITAL VISITORS AND RESIDENTS

A concept developed by David White and Alison Le Cornu (White and Le Cornu, 2011) which is used as a framework to understand the engagement of individuals with the **web** and with digital technology in general. Broadly speaking, digital visitors tend to use the technology for specific short-term purposes and leave a low 'footprint', whereas digital residents tend to have a high number of online connections and be quite visible on the web and **social media**, such as through **blogging** and presence on **Facebook**, or through **Twitter**. Contrasts with the concept of **digital natives and immigrants**.

DIGITIZING

The act of electronically copying printed material into a digital format, usually for dissemination to remote learners via a **VLE** or **MLE**. A common use is for academic papers and/or chapters of textbooks to be digitized and included as relevant reading material on **distributed education** courses where learners do not have ready access to a large conventional library. Digitized copies of articles may be stored on secure sites that require **password** access, such as an institutional VLE, some **online libraries** or subject-related portals that are related to educational purposes. Digitization has the advantage of making high-quality resources (including hard-to-get and out-of-print materials) available to a geographically distributed group of learners, but it is subject to the usual restrictions on **copyright** and **plagiarism**.

DISCUSSION BOARD

A variation of a bulletin board system that allows learners and tutors to engage in an extended, structured dialogue on topics of relevance to their course of study. Most **VLEs** and **MLEs** have discussion boards as part of their structural components, and they are frequently crucial in establishing the level of group **interaction** that leads to the formation of **online** learning **communities** and **feedback** from both staff and fellow learners. Due to the fundamental importance of discussion boards in stimulating interaction, and due to the importance of this interaction in promoting deeper levels of learning, some tutors allocate marks to students for the quality and quantity of their **postings** to the course discussion board. In this way, the discussion board can be used as an educational forum for learners – as an important way of encouraging learners to engage with other sources of learning materials, and also as a means of **assessment** of the level of engagement of the student with the learning process.

DISTRIBUTED EDUCATION

Amongst the terms that are being used to describe forms of learning in **online** and mixed delivery format, or simply educational delivery that is different from the 'traditional' approach, the concept of distributed learning is increasingly finding favour. Part of the appeal of this concept is that it is vaguely descriptive and so appears to cover a variety of circumstances, while at the same time being specific enough to convey the idea that it is not simply referring to single-location **face-to-face** (**f2f**) delivery. The 'distributed' description applies mainly to a) a form of distance education that is delivered across a wide geographical area, perhaps to multi-site campuses and/or local learning centres; and b) a form of **blended learning** in which the teaching and learning resources are distributed across a range of media types and communication styles.

The intention of the term is to describe the process rather than a particular theory of learning, and it usually refers to a form of educational delivery that is distributed in the context of *both* location and learning resources. In relation to the location of students, blended learning implies that both campus-based students and those who are at remote sites from the **tutoring** are able to access the same **modules** and courses, perhaps as part of the same 'class' but certainly over the same time duration. In practice, these learners may be scattered across a number of learning centres, partner colleges or, in some cases, individual homes or workplaces. There is no rule to differentiate whether they are distributed over three separate sites or 300.

Similarly, the concept of 'distributed resources' conveys an explicit understanding that a wide variety of **courseware**, learning styles, resources, communication tools and types of **assessment** will be employed in the educational provision. A practical example might be of a module on a degree programme that is delivered to students on the same campus as the tutor, but also to thirty or forty other locations. Some of the students may choose to visit another college in the **network** or drop into a local learning centre for specific study tasks.

All of the learners are joined through the same **VLE** and access the course in an **asynchronous** manner over the same semester. Learners at the main campus or subsidiary colleges may choose to borrow books from the library of that institution, while those studying from work or home may place a greater reliance on access to online articles and journals. Some students may prefer to visit local learning centres in order to use restricted portals giving access to specialist academic publications that the institution subscribes to, or to use special equipment such as **videoconference** facilities or complex **software** shared over **broadband**. Students on the main campus may elect to meet face-to-face with their course tutor to discuss set topics, while others in more remote locations may prefer to **audioconference, videoconference** or speak to their tutor by **email**, ordinary telephone calls, or through applications such as **instant messaging** or other **web** meetings. Although the greater emphasis on flexibility is generally positive, this needs to be balanced with the added costs of providing very similar educational materials in different formats for perhaps relatively small numbers of students, and this is an important consideration in the **course design** of distributed education.

DOMAIN NAME

Quite simply, this is the common 'address' on the **web** to allow users to locate an individual **webpage**. Web locations will also have a technical, digital numerical, identifier known as the IP (Internet Protocol) address, but these tend to be more clumsy and difficult to remember. A typical domain name will combine a unique combination of identification to locate the host **server** computer in an **internet** search. Examples are normally prefixed by 'www' (standing for 'world wide web') and appear in the form www.uhi.ac. uk or www.bbc.co.uk where 'uhi' stands for University of the Highlands and Islands, and 'bbc' denotes the British Broadcasting Corporation. The suffix 'ac' indicates an academic institution and 'uk' locates the country of registration. Other indicators include 'org' for an organisation, and 'com' for a company. Usually the root domain name indicates the **homepage** of the organisation, with additional webpages built up by adding extensions to the link, such as https://www.uhi.ac.uk/en/campuses/

DOMAIN OF ONE'S OWN (DOOO)

Originating within the University of Mary Washington in 2012, Domain of One's Own is a philosophy and approach which supports and empowers students, and academics, in owning and maintaining a personal **domain name** and associated web space. Key aspects of the philosophy of DoOO include: students, and academics, owning but also understanding how to own, control maintain and grow their own web domain. It requires users to develop their **digital literacies** and capabilities in doing so, and to retain and exercise ownership and capacity to digitally curate, distribute and allow access to their own intellectual work, scholarship and data during and beyond their course of studies, and beyond their time as a student or academic at a particular university. Jim Groom was one of the key figures in the development of DoOO at the University of Mary Washington, and he has extended the concept to the wider academic community through his Reclaim Hosting organisation. An increasing number of universities worldwide are also engaging in their own DoOO initiatives.

DOWNLOAD

To download is to transfer data onto a PC from another computer or **network**. This term is often confused with the term **upload**, as the information that a user downloads onto their own computer has frequently been uploaded to the network by another user somewhere else. The speed of the download is governed both by the size and complexity of the data files being transferred and also by the **bandwidth** available to the user. Generally speaking, small, simple files can be downloaded quite quickly on most modern machines, but larger files, or complex data such as **graphics**, interactive maps, **video clips** and **software** may need higher-bandwidth connections (so-called **broadband**) in order to download them with a reasonable speed and accuracy. Slow download times are a source of frustration for many elearners, and it is not uncommon for the computer screen to 'freeze' or disconnect entirely if the **internet** connection is overloaded. For this reason, course designers need to take care in the construction of their **MLE** course sites that no unnecessary graphics or very large text files are included without either giving learners sufficient warning or giving them the option/choice to download or not. In **distributed education**, some courses may include these large or complex files on a CD in order to overcome the need for students to download large quantities of data over mediocre internet connections.

DROPBOX

A **software** facility of many types of **VLE** or **MLE** that allows elearners to submit their **assessment** materials (usually anonymously) for marking by their course tutor. Learners send their pieces of work to the dropbox in a manner similar to sending an **email** with an **attachment**, and depending on the sophistication of the VLE or MLE a message will be sent to one marker (or more) and a receipt of acknowledgement will be sent to the learner. Tutors can then recover the submitted pieces of work after the assignment deadline by accessing a special, **password** protected area of the MLE. The dropbox has an advantage over assignments that are simply emailed to tutors in that they can preserve the anonymity of the students until the work has been marked and tutors are ready to give **feedback** to the learners.

ECDL (EUROPEAN COMPUTER DRIVING LICENCE)

This is an internationally recognised qualification in computer competency covering various aspects such as basic file-management, word-processing, spreadsheets, **database** management, **email** and **web**, and presentations. The certificate based upon relating practical applications to theory is designed as a benchmark qualification for computer users, especially those with a need to demonstrate their competence for the advancement of their career.

EDUTAINMENT

This is a portmanteau word, bringing together 'education' and 'entertainment'. It specifically refers to programmes or activities that use forms of mass entertainment to introduce opportunities for public education in a non-formal manner. Although its use has a relatively long history on radio (e.g. *The Archers*) and on television (e.g. *Blue Peter* and *Sesame Street*), each of which have been successfully used to incorporate educational messages and activities for the mass audience, there has been a very slow uptake in formal higher education.

In **gamification**, the rapid growth of digital games as a hobby and the continuing spread of elearning has encouraged some educators to combine elements of the two in order to stimulate greater **interaction** with learning materials, particularly amongst young learners. The incorporation of elements such as quizzes on the **VLE** or **MLE** to provide self-test opportunities and/or formative **assessment** and to give quick **feedback** to learners has resulted in a number of educational games that include, for instance, **multiple choice questions (MCQs)**.

The concept has much in common with 'infotainment' a portmanteau term that combines 'information' and 'entertainment' in a manner that seeks to make news and current affairs items appear entertaining to a wider demographical market sector. Both terms seek to reach out in an informal manner to new client groups that traditional forms of education (or news coverage) have failed to engage with and/or who are apparently less able to take advantage of more traditional learning methods. Edutainment is of course not restricted to **online** varieties, and it has been possible to combine educational games (e.g. business games) with other learning resources to utilise the social learning aspect of the games in a form of **distributed education**.

EMAIL

Email messages are usually text sent from one person to another via computer. Email can also be sent automatically to a large number of addresses. In elearning, email has several uses: one-to-one communication between, say, student and tutor, and one-to-many communication from, say, the tutor to all the students in the group. Most **VLEs** have a separate email facility for messages that are personal or not relevant to the whole group.

EMOTICONS

The reliance of **email**, and other forms of CMC, on the written word, is often thought to cause a very concise, even terse, dialogue between users, which is frequently misinterpreted as brusqueness or rudeness. Occasionally these comments may lead to **flaming or flame wars** requiring time and patience to resolve. As a consequence of this, some users include emoticons in their text (shorthand for 'emotional **icons**') to indicate the spirit in which their message is sent. Examples might include the familiar smiley face :o) to indicate a joking remark and corresponding variations for sadness :-(or for confusion :o/, and so on. Some newer applications such as **instant messaging** software may include a range of customised emoticons to encourage non-verbal cues to be included within **text messages**.

ENCRYPTION

The practice of encrypting digital information or data, such as a file, **database, text message**, or **password**, involves converting it into an unrecognised form or code so that it may only be viewed by authorised users using authorised programmes or applications. Encryption is routinely used to secure data and information sent via the **internet** or **wireless networks**.

EPORTFOLIO

Electronic portfolios (also referred to as eportfolios or webfolios) are increasingly recognised as a valuable tool not only for learners but also for instructors and academic organisations. Eportfolio implementation is a major development area in elearning. Three categories of use can be distinguished, though the boundaries are not clear-cut. Eportfolios are used:

- for **assessment**;
- as a form of personal development planning for staff and students;
- as a tool to support reflection on learning and teaching.

The growth of eportfolios is fuelled by a number of broad factors: the dynamics of functioning in a knowledge economy, the changing nature of learning and the changing needs of the learner. One way of describing them might be, 'a dynamic, ever-growing, annotated CV'.

An 'idealised' scenario for the use of an eportfolio by a student would be: the student enters each item as a unique object with **metadata** to enable easy access; the items can be grouped and permissions granted for different audiences. For assessment purposes, the learner draws items from the bank of items and sends a link to the instructor; for employment purposes, the learner chooses items which show a required skill.

One of the anticipated benefits of eportfolios is that they should facilitate the process of learners being able to make connections between learning experiences, especially between formal and informal experiences. They should also provide the metacognitive elements learners require to plan future learning needs based on their previous successes and failures.

Eportfolios, as opposed to portfolios, are still in the expansion and experiment phase of development. However, it is possible to summarise current uses for students as follows:

- The eportfolio is embedded into the curriculum as a tool to support learning;
- There is a strong emphasis on supporting reflection on learning;
- There is an intention to encourage students to take responsibility for their own learning.

Despite these uses, persuading students of the potential benefits and of the need to take seriously the business of continually updating their portfolio is something of an uphill struggle. Some universities are now offering credit for the recording and reflection aspects of eportfolio development.

For academic staff, eportfolio updating may well be mandatory and related to promotion and salary increases. An academic eportfolio might consist of a résumé, a statement of teaching philosophy, examples of teaching practice (such as **course design, feedback** from students or extracts from **interactions** with students) and reflective processes which demonstrate professional growth.

Many universities that have embedded eportfolios into the curriculum have done so in a way that enables assessment for learning by means of inbuilt, **online**, instantaneous feedback systems. Assessment which consists of the student selecting pieces of work and providing a linking overview is a more common use of the portfolio concept. Another aspect of assessment is self-assessment and this practice is strongly associated with the introduction of eportfolios. For example, students might be asked to reflect on their learning and to diagnose their strengths and weaknesses. This regular reflection process then forms part of their eportfolio. Students might also be expected to identify two or three skills or areas of study they would like to develop, and accompanying this would be their plan of action for accomplishing this development. In short, an eportfolio in an educational context consists of an archive of past work, evidence of current activities, assessment and reflection, plus plans for the future. It is apparent that students need advice and support from tutors and mentors to carry out this level of **self-directed learning**.

The process of creating an eportfolio consists of collecting pieces of work, assessments, presentations, websites, blogs, etc., explaining how the learning experiences relate to course content or learning objectives, and documenting this with evidence from the pieces submitted. Students can share their eportfolios with staff and/or other students, who can add their comments.

While new 'purpose-built' eportfolio **software** is available commercially, many users have built systems using existing software, such as **HTML** editors – Dreamweaver or FrontPage – web design tools such as Flash and Authorware, blogs and **Wikis**, and, finally, content management systems. One of the areas of eportfolio development is the integration of **blogging** and eportfolio **software**, thus underlining the aim of eportfolios to support reflection and self-directed learning.

E-TEXTBOOKS

Short for 'electronic textbooks', these are digital versions of the conventional paper-based books, although they have additional features, such as the ability to search the book for key terms, the inclusion of **hyperlinks** to other **webpages** and **animations**. E-books are different from documents such as **PDFs** in that they can incorporate functions such as the ability to change the font size (which automatically re-sizes the pages) and can be used in real time by multiple users at the same time. E-books require an electronic reader, such as a **tablet** or a Kindle, or can be read directly **online** or as a **download** from the **web**.

EXPERIENTIAL LEARNING

This is a theory of adult education and **lifelong learning** that suggests learners acquire knowledge and skills in a more profound manner when they are actually engaged with the subject matter, rather than considering it at a distance or in an abstract form. The emphasis upon individuals having a direct experience of the learning materials means that experiential learning is not restricted to the formal education system, and indeed some educationalists have argued that in its most pure form, the learning experiences should directly relate to events in the life of the individual learner.

The ability for elearners to have heightened **interaction** with other learners (both globally and over time) using electronic means such as **email**, a **VLE** and/or other forms of **distributed education** suggests that there are rich opportunities to share experiences with other elearners in an informal but structured way. In this process, learners can share experiences, reflect upon the discussions in the light of their own experience, form and test concepts or ideas in a concrete manner (e.g. by carrying out a subsequent activity), and then observe and reflect upon their new experiences arising from that activity. The process is therefore circular and potentially endless, frequently summarised by Kolb's learning cycle, although this theory is not without its critics.

FACE-TO-FACE (F2F)

With the evolution of **distributed education** and a wide variety of different ways to make contact between individuals and groups who are geographically dispersed, the term 'face-to-face', or simply 'f2f', has come to refer to meetings that take place in person (i.e. with the participants in the same room). Increasingly, in distributed education it has become necessary to specify a 'f2f meeting' in order to differentiate those meetings from the more common areas of educational **interactivity** such as by **videoconference**, by **audioconference** or through a variety of **computer-mediated conference** styles such as **virtual seminars**, shorter **instant messaging** connections or communication via **software** such as **Skype**.

FACEBOOK

Facebook is a social media site enabling networking with friends and colleagues, including the sharing of **text messaging**, images, **video clips, hyperlinks**, etc. Generally, people 'follow' the **posts** of people in their **networks** and share their data on a reciprocal basis, but there are some controls to restrict access to 'friends', to block unwanted followers and to set up closed groups of 'invitation-only' users. There has been some experimentation to use Facebook in education, but the lack of complete control by users, and the challenges of data control and storage, seem to make this service better for **social networking** rather than for formal education.

FACILITATOR

This is the term used for the **online** tutor who guides and organises discussion. The online environment is much less teacher-centric than the **face-to-face (f2f)** classroom, and the use of 'facilitator' rather than teacher reflects this change in role and power.

FAQs

Frequently Asked Question (FAQ) files are **online** informational lists of common enquiries from users in question-and-answer format. They include standard responses prepared either by the instructor or a technical assistant. The aim is to assist new users and to avoid repetitive offline enquiries. They are often built up through successive presentations of a course.

FEEDBACK

This is a general term used to describe any structured comments, written or verbal, that are given to learners on work that they have submitted for **assessment**. Experience has shown that carefully considered comments from the tutor to the learner on the work being assessed are much more effective in the learning process when they closely follow the submission and marking of the assignment. Most universities have a regulation that states the maximum period allowed for some form of formal feedback on the submitted work of the learner – normally two to three weeks. The transmission of feedback is crucial in helping the learner gain an awareness and appreciation of their strong/weak points, and the reasons for the grade of mark that they have obtained.

Timely and appropriate feedback is especially important in distance education as this may be the only real contact that a learner has with their tutor, and hence the only significant opportunity to learn constructively from any mistakes. In terms of elearning, feedback is also a critical component of the learner-tutor **interaction**. When dealing with learners who are studying at locations remote from the main location of the tutor, these are effectively distance students and have a similar dependence on the speed and quality of tutor feedback as a measure of their progress. This is true even when the learner is participating in **distributed education** and elearning: text-based **online** feedback is only one of the conduits of communication with tutorial staff and other learners. In the situation where elearning is a key component of learning for campus-based students, feedback is no less important, but of course it may be provided by a variety of means, including written comments, **face-to-face** (**f2f**) tutorials and/or seminars.

Feedback frequently follows an unwritten rule that the comments by the tutor should begin by praising some aspect of the submitted work, followed by carefully worded comments identifying the main aspects that could be improved to obtain a higher mark, and finishing by making some positive suggestions as to how the learner could build on this to improve future performance. The scope of the feedback can be very narrow or very wide ranging according to the subject and the level, and it usually covers such items as developing an argument, proper referencing, developing critical thinking, providing evidence for assertions, deepening knowledge and generally improving the communication skills of the learner. As with other aspects of elearning, feedback to students provided electronically by **email** or through a subject **discussion board** can frequently be used to dramatic effect due to the speed and immediacy of the media. The introduction of new technological applications such as **instant messaging**, and connections by **Skype** and/or **videoconference** into elearning practice, offer opportunities for more or less immediate feedback to learners even if they are widely scattered geographically.

In practice, there is no difference between feedback that is given for formative assessments and that which is given for a summative assessment and final grade, but there may be a great deal of difference in the way these are treated by the educational establishment and, correspondingly, in their impact on the learner. Feedback on formative assessments allows the learner to build up a good picture of how well they are performing and what areas require improving before the submission of the final summative assessment so critical for the final grade. On the other hand, providing feedback only on the summative assessment means that a learner does not have the opportunity to improve on subsequent assessment. For this reason, some educators have developed the practice of providing 'concurrent feedback' intermittently during assessments, and again this style has translated very effectively to elearning in general. (It is easy for students to submit drafts to the tutor to check that they are on the right track.) Key factors in providing good feedback are:

- It should compare the performance of the learner with some other performance of an appropriate (good) standard;
- It provides guidance and cites evidence for the tutor's comments;
- It is presented to the learner in a timely manner;
- The advice is useable and clearly explained;

- It presents suggestions, and perhaps further reading, to allow the learner to improve on their performance;
- It clearly relates the learner's performance to the grade acquired.

In some instances, and at some levels of undergraduate studies, feedback can be given immediately to elearners by the use of online **multiple choice questionnaires** (**MCQs**) that have been written to give an automatic response. In these cases, the selection of a wrong answer will not only indicate the error immediately to the learner but will explain why this selection is incorrect. The choice of a correct answer will also provide some further detail and will allow the learner to proceed to the next question, providing an overall grade at the end if required. Some educationalists dislike MCQ as an assessment option, claiming that it promotes superficial as opposed to deep learning, but in elearning they have frequently been included as short in-text tests of student understanding of topics on the **MLE**, to provide some formative self-assessment and quick, constructive feedback.

FILE TRANSFER PROTOCOL (FTP)

A computer agreement protocol that enables entire files to be transferred between one computer and another over the **internet**.

FIREWALL

A firewall is a piece of **software** and/or **hardware** used to provide security within and between computer **networks**. In general, a firewall provides network security to users **online** and defines the zone of **trust** that exists within **communities**, from the open access free-for-all of the **internet** to the relatively safe environment of an organisational **intranet**. A firewall filters out unwelcoming and hostile communications and prevents other networks gaining access to a private network if they do not have the necessary permissions.

FLAMING (OR FLAME WAR)

This refers to an exchange of intemperate, hostile or abusive messages via electronic media, such as **discussion boards**, by **instant messaging** or by group **email**. The immediacy of these media, together with the tendency for them to be text-based and relatively short, has given rise to a tendency for users to respond quickly to previous messages. In some cases, the brevity of the response, coupled with the lack of detailed ways to convey emotion, can produce seemingly strong feelings which can escalate quickly into heated **online** exchanges, or flame wars. New elearners, especially, are encouraged to pause for thought before replying to provocative messages, and more frequent users often resort to **emoticons** to give the suggestion of their humour in the context of the message. Flaming is the online equivalent to an explosive outburst in a **face-to-face** (**f2f**) meeting, and while this may sometimes provoke a useful exchange of radically different opinions, its continued use is not to be recommended or tolerated by the responsible **moderator**.

FLEXIBLE LEARNING

This term is used most commonly in Australia, though not exclusively there. Flexible learning is very close in meaning to '**open learning**' as both are focused on the ability for learners to decide what, where, when and how they learn. Elearning is considered to be a component of flexible learning or possibly one type of flexible learning. In Australia, the term is used in relation to both vocational programmes and higher education, whereas in the UK it is primarily used in reference to further rather than higher education.

A **student-centred** approach to education underpins the concept of flexible learning. The following characteristics of flexible learning indicate a strong similarity with distance education and elearning. For example:

- Flexible learning relies less on **face-to-face** (**f2f**) teaching and more on guided independent learning – teachers become **facilitators** of the learning process directing students to appropriate resources, tasks and learning outcomes;

- Flexible learning places greater reliance on high-quality learning resources using a range of technologies (e.g. print, CD-ROM, video, audio, the **internet**);
- Flexible learning provides opportunities to communicate outside traditional teaching times;
- Flexible learning makes use of **ICT** and multi-skilled teams to produce, deliver, teach and administer the courses.

As with elearning, IT is often central to much of the implementation of flexible learning; for example, in delivering learning resources, providing a communications facility, administering units and student **assessment**, and hosting student support systems. Related to this is the use of teams rather than individual academics undertaking all stages of unit planning, development, delivery, assessment and maintenance. Instead, other professionals are often required to provide specific skills; for example, in **instructional design**, desktop publishing, **web** development, and administration and maintenance of programmes.

As with **open learning**, flexible learning is an aspiration or aim, rather than a method of education. The aspiration is to provide access and equity; in other words, to reduce or eliminate any barriers that stand between the learner and the learning environment. Examples of barriers are: previous qualifications, geographical location, lifestyle and ability to pay. It is rare to find an accredited programme that removes all barriers. Totally flexible learning would include:

- open entry with no prerequisite qualifications required;
- multiple annual start dates;
- both time and location of study determined by the student;
- the pace of progress through the course determined by the student;
- assessment and content of the course negotiated by the student;
- no cost to the student for studying the course.

It is questionable whether any such programme, if it did exist, would have enough structure, dynamism and challenge to be successful. In short, some flexibility is good, but more is not necessarily better.

Three educational principles are evident in most programmes that aim to be flexible: opportunities to learn by doing, opportunities to contextualise learning and individual **feedback** to learners on their work. Of course, these principles are not unique to flexible learning; arguably they should underpin all forms of teaching and learning.

Learning by doing is particularly relevant for vocational programmes, but it is appropriate at all educational levels. Even textbooks and other print material should contain tasks and activities, with answers preferably at the back. Although print is a more flexible medium, computer-based materials can be more motivating, interactive and dynamic than print.

Flexible learning should offer students the opportunity to tailor some or all of the learning content, process, outcomes or assessment to their individual circumstances. For example, an assessment could allow students to apply the topic to their employment or desired employment. The content of the course could offer students the possibility of studying in depth the aspects of the subject that most interest them.

The benefit to learners of detailed, sympathetic and timely feedback on submitted work cannot be over-estimated. Students who return to formal education after some time usually need reassurance, praise for what is good in their work, and careful but honest feedback on what needs to be improved. Most important is specific advice on how to improve.

An aspect of flexibility that is highly valued by non-traditional students is the facility for recognition of prior learning. This allows students to prepare a case demonstrating what they have learned from employment or other experience and submit this for consideration for partial credit towards a degree. Related to this facility is the possibility of transferring credits gained from one institution to another. Because of employment moves, family and various kinds of personal crises, the need for students to gain their degree from a number of institutions is a growing phenomenon.

As with distance education and elearning, flexible delivery requires more planning before the course begins. The course designers need to consider developing or providing a range of additional material to the core content of the course. Background material might be necessary, as students will not all have the same starting knowledge. Remedial material might also be needed for students lacking particular skills. Finally, experienced course designers know how important clarity is in all instructions and assessment questions. When opportunities for face-to-face clarification are few, it is essential to prevent confusion by careful presentation in the first place. One way of doing this is to pilot materials with potential or actual students. Through feedback or observation, course designers can build up their expertise in how to write clearly and in what kinds of problems students have with course content.

Flexible delivery of education has two components: enhancing the educational experience for learners and widening participation in education to those normally excluded.

FOLKSONOMY

This is a system of the classification of data by adding tags so that the items can be labelled for subsequent search, retrieval and sharing. The tagging is often done **online** through public **accessibility** by making the tags visible to users of a **network** service. Common examples might include the **tagging** of images/photographs, **social bookmarking** of interesting **webpages**, and the sharing of **learning objects** to enhance **collaborative learning/work** activities.

GAMIFICATION

Jisc (2016) defines 'gamification' as 'where techniques or approaches from games are adopted or incorporated into non-gaming activities to make them more engaging or enjoyable', providing examples of gamification in teaching and learning that include:

- Using **[digital badges]** or other rewards to record achievements;
- Encouraging progression through tasks by offering progress markers;
- Including competitive elements and rankings;
- Game-based learning or **'serious games'** – these are educational games designed to fulfil a particular curriculum need.

Gamification within educational activities will often involve means for individuals to gauge their progress against their peers, as indicated above, in addition to **collaborative learning** opportunities involving problem-solving, immediate **feedback**, and a designed progression in level of challenge, difficulty or complexity. Increased **motivation**, engagement, and enjoyment within educational tasks and activities are often associated with gamified elements and approaches. Poor applications of gamification principles in learning and **learning design** may result in 'trivialising' educational tasks and activities, and many leading proponents of gamification in learning and digital education provide guidance on how to avoid this.

GIF

This stands for 'graphics interchange format' and refers to a specific type of computer file used especially with **webpages** for transferring **graphics** easily between computers and across **networks**. A GIF file is compressed to reduce the size of the file without losing any visual accuracy, but the restriction to 256 colours means that they are better for diagrams and simple **web** images but are not usually used to transfer photographs.

See also: **JPEG**.

GRAPHICS

Any image, diagram, or illustration that is reproduced in digital format and used to elaborate a **webpage** or another computer file can be considered a graphic. Graphics can be used as simple decoration and/or can function as **hyperlinks** to navigate to another **internet** locations. Due to the complexity of the data stored, graphics can take up a large amount of computer memory, and they will also take a long time to **download** for a user with a low-**bandwidth** connection to the internet. For this reason, graphics should be used carefully, whether on a webpage or embedded in another document, such as a word-processed file. Frustration in attempting to view or download large graphics files is a frequent cause of elearner dissatisfaction with **online** resources, and it is good design practice to bring such large files to the attention of the learner (e.g. 'the graphic at this link is 7KB') and either open them on a different webpage window or as an **attachment** such as a **JPEG** file.

GROUPWORK

Many educators regard this as one of the mainstays of **online** courses. Group assignments and meetings can be facilitated by **email**, private **chatrooms, discussion boards** and voice calls. There are pitfalls, however, to the use of groupwork: many people are antagonistic and resent others in the group who do not 'pull their weight'; different learning styles and study patterns can make the work difficult to coordinate, and group marks can be contentious. Solutions include: building more measures that support positive interdependence, individual accountability and collaborative skills; increasing opportunities for the socio-emotional and affective exchanges between learners; adjusting the tutor's and the learners' roles for CSCL environments; and increasing social presence, i.e. reducing the perceived distance between learners.

See also: **collaborative work/learning**.

HACKER

Although this term began simply as a description of someone who is a serious computer programmer, it has evolved to mean a person who uses their programming expertise to 'break through' the security system of computer **networks**. A typical hacker might violate the **firewall** of a **password** protected network in order to gain access to confidential data and/or to advertise the fact that they have been clever enough to break through the organisation's security. A hacker is not the same as a person who creates a **virus** with the deliberate aim of causing damage, and many hackers would now consider themselves to be fighting for the free use of the **internet** against those corporate interests that would like to restrict and control access for commercial benefits.

HARDWARE

This comprises the physical components of a computing system or **network**, such as the computer processing unit itself, together with the screen (or visual display unit) and any other peripheral devices such as a printer, **modem**, audio speakers, **webcam**, external CD drive or cables. Hardware is normally the host or the means for **software** to function; that is to say, software gives the instructions for the hardware to carry out certain tasks, such as printing or displaying information from an **internet** connection.

HASHTAG

A hashtag is a word or phrase (without spaces) prefixed with the # symbol and used on **social networking** sites, including **Twitter**, to allow users to easily identify messages and exchanges that relate to the same topic or event. For example, searching Twitter using the hashtag #blendedlearning would allow the user to see all the publicly posted **Tweets** from users that have featured that particular hashtag to post on the topic of **blended learning**. Similarly, for an event, searching Twitter using the hashtag #Olympics2018 would bring up a listing of all publicly visible Tweets relating to the 2018 Olympic Games. Note that while some hashtags are created using capital letters, hashtags are not case sensitive.

HELPLINE/HELPDESK

As increasing numbers of learners seek access to educational material in an **online** format, and from geographically scattered locations (see **distributed education**), there has been a realisation that some technical assistance is often necessary. A helpdesk usually provides telephone advice from **network** experts, often including an 'out of hours' or 24/7 service to cover generic questions on problems that learners encounter. Typical problems would include learners that have forgotten their **password** or have difficulty in connecting to the institutional **VLE** or **MLE**, or perhaps those who have difficulty in navigating the VLE to locate the **discussion board** or other component relevant to their studies. The value of the helpdesk is that it uses simple, immediate technology (e.g. a telephone) to connect people who have a problem, *when* they have the problem, to a specialist who can log their call and either provide an immediate answer or else connect them to a relevant specialist who will make contact. Although it seems that many of the helpdesk enquiries are relatively trivial, there is a great comfort factor for novice elearners in knowing that help is only a phone call away.

HEUTAGOGY

This is a common feature of **online learning**, covering learners who **surf** for **open educational resources** and those who use **open access** courses to study for pleasure or simply to study at their own convenience. Although the term '**pedagogy**' is now commonly used to refer to the theory and practice of education, it literally translates to 'leading children'. '**Andragogy**' is the preferred term for some theorists and practitioners to refer to the theory and practice of adult education. The term 'heutagogy' has a distinct meaning in referring to the theory, study and practice of self-determined learning.

The emphasis on self-determined, rather than self-directed, learning is an important one as heutagogical principles espouse the importance and development of autonomy, competency and capability, self-efficacy, and communicative skills and ability, with the end goal of enabling effective **lifelong learning** and adaptability to new contexts. In heutagogical approaches to formal education, the tutor's role is almost exclusively a coaching one with the student identifying their own problems, challenges or paths of inquiry to tackle or pursue within the broad parameters of curricula which are domain specific but largely negotiable in relation to how the individual will learn, what they will focus upon and how they will evidence their learning. There are strong links between heutagogy as defined above and **constructivism**, between heutagogy and some of the key assumptions of **connectivism**, and between heutagogy and the kinds of engagement expected of learners in **MOOCs**. There may be a continuum with **andragogy**, but heutagogy can apply to all categories of learning, structured or unstructured, with both **digital visitors and residents**.

HOMEPAGE

This is the opening page of a series of pages on the **web**. The homepage usually is the reference location of the **web presence** of an individual or organisation and is identified by a **URL**. Normally the homepage will contain a number of **hyperlinks** to other

webpages and is used as a 'shop window' to display other resources that the owners of the webpage want to bring to the attention of the user. The homepage can be considered the root page of a complex website, and users can navigate their way through a large variety of other web-based resources by using the homepage as a navigational point, usually by clicking on a button labelled 'home' to return to the opening page.

HTML

Hyper Text Markup Language (HTML) is a language used to create a **webpage** that allows text, **graphics** and other information to be viewed through a **browser**. At its simplest, this consists of a series of commands that are used to identify headings, font sizes, colours and links to other sites that are incorporated into the design of the webpage. In conventional use, most users will not see these commands, as they remain hidden in the final screen presentation. Users can view the HTML structure of a specific webpage by going to that page then selecting <view> then <source> from the **toolbar** at the top of the screen. Initially HTML was presented in a very loose structure that was interpreted by the web browser, but increasingly strict rules of construction have been applied to govern the language and control more accurately what the **web** designer wishes to express. Some early examples of elearning courses were simply word documents that were converted into HTML and displayed for open access on the **web**. With increasing sophistication, these early attempts were replaced by customised elearning **platforms** and **VLEs**, which gave greater control over the structure and content of the site but restricted access to authorised users with an institutional **password**. There is a move towards XHTML (Extensible Hyper Text Markup Language) that is similar in structure but with a stricter syntax that will allow for a flexible use of common standards across the various machine-readable communications systems using the **internet**.

The first few lines of HTML for a website, may e.g. read as follows,

```
<html>
<head>
Welcome to UHI Millennium Institute – &quot;Creating the University of the Highlands &amp; Islands&quot;
<meta http-equiv="Content-Type"content="text/html; charset=iso-8859-1">
<script language="JavaScript1.2"src="includes/browsercheck.js">
</script>
```

HTTP

Hypertext Transfer Protocol (HTTP) was designed to allow publication of materials on the World Wide **Web**. This is a method of request and response for communicating information across the **internet** in a standard manner that allows users to send documents and other digital information between computers. It follows a standard set of rules for data identification, **authentication** and error correction, and uses **hypertext** as a means of cross-referencing documents to allow users to access layers of different information from different sources upon request. These documents can be held on a computer anywhere in the world that acts as a **server** to supply documents as **webpages** to users over the internet.

HYPER-INTERACTIVITY

Due to the increasing speed of **internet** access, and the extensive range of inter-connected **network** services, it is now possible not only to interact very quickly one-to-one with distant users of **email, webpages** and **social media** but also to one-to-many and many-to-many. This allows news, ideas, images and video to be circulated globally in seconds with a speed never before achievable.

HYPERLINK/HYPERTEXT

A line of text, a **graphic** or an **icon** on a **webpage** that provides a link to another webpage or **web**-based resource when the user clicks on it with the computer mouse. Hyperlinks (whether they are text or images) are constructed using **HTML** that enables identification and visual display when used with a **browser** to navigate a path through the resources on the **internet**. Commonly, hypertext is displayed on a webpage in a different colour from the main text and is underlined and/or in bold. Moving the cursor over a hyperlink usually causes the cursor to change from an arrow to a hand with a pointing finger to indicate a link to another 'layer' of resources.

ICON

An image that stands as a symbol and is used in computing to indicate an activity or a location to the user of a particular piece of **software**. An example might be a picture of a folder to indicate a location in which to store files; a representation of a filing cabinet to indicate a location to store electronic folders or documents; or a picture of a printer to indicate the command button to print a current document. Common icons are usually displayed in the **toolbar** of a software application, or on the **desktop** of the user's computer.

ICT

Used as a common abbreviation for 'information and communications technology', this is a very broad descriptive term for any **hardware** or **software**, or even any activity, that is related to the use of computers for the generation, storage, transmission and retrieval of information in an electronic format. Early forms of the concept often referred simply to 'information technology' (IT) but the additional component of rapid digital transfer of information between computers in a **network**, and using computers to communicate by **email**, or **videoconferencing** on the **desktop**, over the **internet**, has substantially enlarged the generic use of the term.

A significant distinction to emerge in recent years is that, as **software** and the **MLE** for elearning has become more sophisticated and 'user friendly', learners no longer need to be highly skilled computer programmers in order to use elearning tools and benefit from the educational experience. This has been summed up in the belief that ICT should *support* learners to do the activities that they choose, rather than be the driving factor that *leads* learners to follow the demands of the hardware and software. There is an implicit assumption that a good use of ICT, combined with good elearning **course design**, will encourage the learner to engage with the learning resources and activities rather than with the ICT.

INSTANT MESSAGING

This is a form of electronic messaging similar to **email** but differing in that the communication takes place as a **synchronous** exchange (i.e. in real time). Many **ISPs** now offer an instant messaging service that allows users of the **network** to identify when colleagues are **online**, enabling them to send and receive short messages immediately. Increasing **convergence** is now encouraging some instant messaging providers to combine with other applications to send **video clips** and voice-over-internet protocol (**VoIP**) as well as conventional **text messages**.

The immediacy of instant messaging has encouraged its use in **distributed education** solutions as a useful means of contact between tutors and students who are remote from the teaching campus. Typically, if a student is on the **web** and is working through some course material but has a problem or question, s/he will notice from a screen **icon** whether the tutor (or a fellow student on their course) is also **online** and can send a short message asking for clarification/explanation. The message is received almost immediately and may result in a quick reply. In supporting online learners, instant messaging usually results in short bursts of text dialogue between two or three individuals in relation to a specific issue, and is therefore a useful means of providing academic guidance when and where it is most needed. Its limitations are that it is restricted to synchronous communications and that it is best for short, concentrated bursts of specific dialogue, in contrast to the depth of reflectivity that is afforded by email and thematic **discussion boards**.

INSTRUCTIONAL DESIGN

A phrase used mainly in the US referring to **course design**.

INTERACTION

Typologies and definitions of **online** interaction have been the subject of much elearning research. Some of the literature distinguishes between interaction with the computer and interaction with other people through the computer. Some research restricts the term 'interaction' to communication with other learners, whereas other research identifies many ways of interacting online: with the interface, with the content, with the tutor and with other students. Where interaction is seen as a complex interplay of many kinds of online activity, the key components are: **course design**, learner engagement, tutor inputs and **platform** capabilities. Many elearning researchers have concluded that social interactions play a major part in increasing the total interaction of an online course and can enhance and further learning.

There is little doubt amongst researchers that the quality of online interaction is an important element in successful elearning. A number of studies have correlated student satisfaction and achievement with interaction levels. Others have shown that students' perceived learning in online courses was related to the level of interaction with the tutor and amongst the students. Furthermore, the quantity of interaction on elearning courses has been shown to be much higher than in **face-to-face** (**f2f**) courses. The quality and usefulness of online interactions, however, are the crucial elements, not the quantity.

At its best, online interaction is knowledge building: students explore issues, examine one another's arguments, agree, disagree and question positions. This kind of interaction contributes to higher order learning through cognitive restructuring or conflict resolution. New ways of understanding the material emerge as a result of contact with different perspectives. Interaction with course content and resource material can also have similar effects. A simple interaction might be an online search to find learning materials or a spreadsheet calculation to solve a problem. A more complex interaction might be a **simulation** or **role play** that enables the learner to explore a problem or **case study** and come to a solution in a non-directed manner. Whether the interaction is with other learners or with content, what makes the difference to the learning outcome is the level of the learner's engagement with the ideas.

A number of researchers have demonstrated that social interaction fosters instructional interaction. Students need to feel comfortable about interacting with their peers, and social exchanges are perceived as safer than discussions about course ideas as the group begins the process of getting to know each other. For this reason, most course designers set up areas for social interaction and include activities, particularly at the beginning of the course, to build social presence and **community**.

Related to social interaction is the expression of emotion, feelings and mood. Novices to the online environment expect interaction to be cold and dry. In fact, the opposite is usually the case. Elearning groups often contain exchanges that are warm, close and welcoming.

One of the difficulties with online interaction that sometimes arises in elearning contexts is that all of the messages are excessively polite. This does not create a stimulating learning environment. The tutor needs to step in and model appropriate processes of questioning and challenging.

The following ways of encouraging online interaction are commonly cited:

1. Timely and personal **feedback** from the tutor on learner contributions and questions.
2. Course design which involves highly interactive activities that are designed to encourage, support and even require interaction.
3. Allocating students to small groups of about six or seven to carry out activities and engage in discussion.
4. Course design which includes combinations of voluntary and required responses, and both initiation of and response to messages.
5. Collaborative activities which require collaborations within and amongst groups.
6. Reinforcement by the tutor of the positive aspects of students' work, which has been shown to lead to improved interaction and subsequently to improved learning.

While some online tutors are concerned with increasing interaction, others are overwhelmed by it, especially when students continue to see the tutor as the 'font of all knowledge'. Techniques commonly cited for tutors to manage online interaction are:

1. Encouraging students to put their queries into the **discussion board** area and not to send **email** unless the communication is very personal.

2. Reducing the level of commenting as the course proceeds, focusing on introducing and summarising discussions.
3. Designing activities in which students take on the role of online **moderator** for short periods.
4. Making clear what the tutorial commitment is, including **logging on** times and frequency.

A few researchers have studied the nature of elearning interactions, and findings across a range of contexts show a surprising degree of consensus. In the majority of messages, students share information and express a point of view. Between 10 and 30 per cent of messages contain expressions of feeling, such as jokes, compliments and self-disclosures. Very few messages contain questions.

Most elearning environments rely on **asynchronous** interaction as the primary means of communication. However, technologies for **synchronous** interaction are developing very quickly and are the focus of experimentation in a number of elearning programmes. Text chat has been available for some time, but multiway audio and video are now available on the **desktop**. Some of the uses for synchronous interaction include: decision-making in the process of collaborative activities, contacting the tutor during office hours and self-help sessions amongst learners. Audio interaction frees learners from typing and allows them to focus on listening, thinking, speaking and questioning. As an occasional supplement to asynchronous interaction, real-time communication provides immediacy and social presence. Students often report that it improves their **motivation** to study.

It is possible to conclude from research into online interaction that the more comfortable students are with the elearning environment, the more likely they are to interact. Complimenting and acknowledging, and expressing appreciation, by both students and tutors are interactive communications that work well in a text-based medium. Tutors and course designers know that when students are interacting well online, the content of the course has been increased in a way that they never could create by other means.

INTERNET

The complex, and rapidly extending, network of interlinked computer **networks** is called the internet. Agreement on a common set of protocols enables computers anywhere in the network to communicate with any other computer in the network, using a wide variety of different paths. Schematically, local area networks (**LANs**) for an organisation or a geographical area are joined together in increasingly larger networks, to give a global coverage. This allows common tasks to be performed throughout the network, such as sending/receiving **email**, or **surfing** the **web** for information (e.g. text or **graphics**) contained in **databases**. The internet enables individuals or organisations to connect web **servers** that host information resources and make these resources available to appropriate users on request.

The structure of the internet allows for secure areas that require a **password** to enter (often requiring payment) and also areas where information is freely available to all. For this reason, the internet is both a wonderful source of detailed information and a source of misinformation or trivia. Learners (formal and non-formal) using the internet must be critically aware of their sources of information and the possibilities for bias and deception. Although there are an increasing number of reliable resources such as peer-reviewed journals (see http://www.irrodl.org/index.php/irrodl and http://www.eurodl.org/) and creditable websites provided by international organisations such as the UN, there is also almost limitless scope for lobbyists, advertising and organisational propaganda. It is crucial that (especially new) learners learn early to distinguish between credible information on the internet and those **webpages** from unverifiable sources.

The internet is able to support a variety of digital devices other than computers and, consequently, provides the central structure for **distributed education** that allows internet connectivity for **videoconferencing**, VoIP telephone conversations, and a variety of **software** applications such as geographical positioning systems or **virtual reality** experiences.

INTERNET CAFÉ

This is a term that has emerged as a generic description of any 'drop-in' facility that provides **internet** access for casual users. Normally a private sector operation, it can also be operated through a local library, tourist bureau, etc. Internet cafés normally charge for use and frequently combine **ICT** access with other commercial activities, such as a bookshop, tourist information, or, as the name suggests, a café.

Internet cafés have frequently developed as a response to the difficulties experienced by mobile users or visitors to an area in obtaining internet access. It is noticeable that in a few areas or countries with exceptionally good internet access, the internet café has been a passing phenomenon as the ubiquity of access reduces the commercial advantage of private businesses. In many rural and remote areas across the world, the internet café has frequently filled the role of a local learning centre for students who either lack access to computing facilities in their home or lack access to specialised equipment (such as a **videoconference** unit) or specialist services (i.e. **broadband** access, or a particular piece of **software**).

The level of sophistication of an internet café may range from simply the basic provision of a self-service computer terminal with internet access to a more highly managed facility that includes technical support and perhaps even basic skills training. Some suppliers have extended their services (particularly in urban areas) to cater for the mobile user by offering internet access via **wireless networks** that allow, for example, business users to conduct informal meetings over coffee in roadside cafés.

The distinction between an internet café and a local learning centre is blurred, with the former being largely a facility for casual or occasional users, whereas a local learning centre generally has a more structured, regular, or formal approach. Some of the more elaborate internet cafés may become 'badged' as learning centres to add marketing value to their profile. An additional educational value of the internet café could be considered to be the social value of providing a gathering place for learners seeking remote access to educational provision, and this has been described as a 'third place' (after home and the workplace) by Oldenberg and others who stress the value of social interaction and group reinforcement that can be provided by learning **communities**, either **online** or in other 'third places' that provide a comfortable networking facility for learners.

INTERNET OF THINGS (IOT)

This involves using the **internet** to interconnect computing devices and computing capabilities within technological appliances (including wearable technology and household appliances) so that they can send share data, communicate and interact. Smart home devices, for example, which allow the control of home services and appliances from a mobile **app**, are one common example of the IOT in practice. In education, a live distributed lab working across multiple sites is enabled by the interconnecting of devices and computing capabilities that is associated with the IOT.

INTERNET SERVICE PROVIDER (ISP)

A company that provides a user with a connection to the **internet**, usually for a cost, though universities and colleges are also ISPs for their students. It is a common complaint from students that when they cease to be students they lose their access to the university/college ISP and, therefore, in their search to find another ISP, frequently lose track of fellow students and access to institutional **online** learning **communities**.

INTRANET

A form of **LAN** that connects the computer systems of a single organisation. An intranet is used to provide common services, such as **email**, access to a common pool of **software** or corporate **webpages**, and uses the same basic structural concepts as the **internet**, with local **clients** and **servers**. An intranet may be connected to the internet (but this is not mandatory), in which case it will normally include a **firewall** to protect the local network from **virus** contamination by external sources. The more sophisticated intranets will allow for different sections to have a different status; for example, there might be some **open access** webpages to provide public guidance or advertising, while senior staff will have access to secure areas that are **password** protected, such as internal email and finance details. Due to the fact that different users can be given different levels of access permissions on an intranet, they can be used effectively to promote **collaborative work**, as well as providing a good base for sharing resources (computer applications, documents, **graphics** or **databases**) as well as providing for **distributed education** in the workplace environment.

JAVA

A particular programming language that is designed to be cross **plat-form**, i.e. it is compatible to run on a variety of computer operating systems, such as Microsoft Windows or Apple MacIntosh. It is currently particularly favoured for its use in constructing certain features of **webpages** (such as **animations** or **multimedia**) as programmers are able to write free-standing applications. These applications are then decoded and run by the machine that accesses the website, rather than the host **server**.

JPEG

This is an acronym for Joint Photographic Experts Group, identifying a specific type of file designed to compress photographs easily for transmission between computers in a **network**, such as the **internet** or an **intranet**. JPEG files usually have the extension .jpg after the file name and are the most common format for the transfer of photographic files over the **web**. The method of compression is best suited for photographs, but not **icons** or other **graphics**, which are more suited to **GIF** format files.

KILLER APP

The 'killer application' has come to mean the 'next big thing' that will achieve a breakthrough to a new level of **ICT** use. It is derived from the observation that an innovative piece of **software** frequently provides the extra marketing incentive that encourages a mass of the public to purchase the supporting **hardware** (e.g. a particular brand of computer or, in **gamification**, a particular brand of handset or control consul). The search for the next killer app has become the next 'best thing' for ICT companies, as widespread public adoption of a new application has frequently led to the generation of considerable wealth and prestige.

LAN (LOCAL AREA NETWORK)

A local area network of computers usually connects a few computers on a small scale, in the home or a workplace. Depending on its purpose, the LAN may or may not be able to connect with other **networks**, e.g. to form a part of the **internet**, by using a router to join wide area networks (WANs). A LAN may form an **intranet** when it is used solely within a single organisation.

LAPTOP

This is a portable computer that can be used while on the move and is suitable for **mobile learning**.

LEARNING DESIGN

This describes the whole process of designing a learning experience that includes not just the methods of engagement with the learner (**face-to-face, online**, or **blended learning**) and more than just the **software**, devices or resources that learners are expected to use, but the entire model of learning that is intended to be employed. Attention to an appropriate learning design is especially crucial in the online environment, firstly because **flexible learning** and **distributed education** require resource preparation to be planned in advance, and, secondly, because in good learning design the educational need should precede the adoption of relevant technology, not vice versa.

Learning design concerns the identification and application of educational approaches and interventions, and the selection or development of corresponding educational resources and technologies, in order to facilitate and support effective learning and teaching. Learning design can be focused on particular activities, on a lesson or series of lessons, or at the level of a unit, course or programme of study, and is cognisant of the level, experience and expected support needs of the intended group of learners, and the knowledge, skills and capabilities that are to be developed.

Learning design is a theoretically grounded, evidence-based process. It involves the application of particular educational concepts and theories in the design and development of learning activities, episodes or curricula, and applying techniques, approaches and technologies for which there is either prior evidence of effectiveness or for which there is evidence of effectiveness from similar or comparable approaches.

Contemporary theory on learning design positions learning design as a 'design science', and offers various means through which to approach the application of learning design principles and the selection of approaches and technologies (e.g. Laurillard, 2012; Goodyear and Dimitriadis, 2013). Within the field of digital education, there are various models and frameworks that guide or have successfully been applied in learning design for blended and online contexts. These include Grainne Conole's 7C's of Learning Design, ABC Learning Design developed by Clive Young and Nataša Perović at UCL, and the 3E Framework.

LEARNING MANAGEMENT SYSTEM (LMS)

'Learning management system' is synonymous with '**MLE**' (managed learning environment) and sometimes also with **VLE** (virtual learning environment). 'LMS' is the term favoured in the US and is often used for provision of corporate training. Whatever the term, the **software** provides a means of administering elearning by providing an access system as well as a tracking system for student progress. Of course, facilities for communication, **assessment** and content display are also part of the **platform**.

LEARNING OBJECTS

Reusable learning objects (RLOs) or just LOs are small units of learning. They have several characteristics which account for the notion that they are a new way of thinking about learning. The first of these is that learning objects are self-contained, that is, they can be studied independently and do not normally refer to other learning objects. This factor leads to the next characteristic: they are reusable in any number of different contexts. LOs can be aggregated into whole courses and can be combined with traditional content. The third important feature of an LO is the use of **metadata**, or **metatagging**, wherein a set of descriptive information about the LO is provided so that **learning object repositories** can be easily searched for appropriate material.

What is the problem to which learning objects are the solution? Many academics think this is still an open question! The obvious answer is that the use of learning objects can reduce duplication of effort in course production. Elearning requires an increase in specially designed learning materials, and high-quality elearning material requires large student numbers or a sizeable budget in order to justify the cost. To address this problem, a number of national and international initiatives have been developed to create digital repositories of learning objects. The vision is that publishers, teachers, support staff, commercial companies and even students would contribute learning objects which could then be easily accessed, recombined, and adapted to different levels and educational models. Examples of such repositories are: CLOE, MERLOT, CAREO, Edutella and The Learning Object Federation.

Repositories are built on **database** technology, but they go beyond a simple storage device. Most encourage discovery, exchange and reuse. As their use expands, it has become apparent that a distributed model linking a range of repositories is a more appropriate scenario. LOs are likely to be stored in any number of places which are all linked by **internet** technology.

Unsurprisingly, there are a number of problems with the reuse of LOs and LO repositories:

1. The issue of combining content from multiple sources.
2. The challenge of developing such flexible content in the first place.
3. The availability of **platforms** to support such use.

In many respects, the vision of LO reuse is a simplistic one, namely: teaching involves the transmission of short blocks of content, and learning is the acquisition of information. The educational process, in most Western universities at least, is much more complex, interactive and supported by human intervention. Learning objects, therefore, even when combined to form a whole course, are in effect a series of resources which need to be supported by activities, **interaction** with tutors and other students, and possibly non-digital learning resources. In addition, the **learning design** of the course needs to be considered right from the start.

In order to be totally flexible, learning objects should be free of context. In theory, that would mean: no reference to any specific discipline, teaching situation or level. This is almost a contradiction in terms, since good teaching is usually considered to be highly adapted to the specific students, subject and context. One solution to this dilemma is to separate the context from the content – not a process teachers are used to performing. This accounts for some of the resistance to learning object reuse by many educators.

In a sense, the metadata attached to each learning object provides one level or type of context. One definition of a learning object is, in fact, data plus context (that is, a resource plus metadata). LO metadata can record the level of difficulty of the resource, the subject matter and its relation to other LOs. If one exercise was designed to follow another, a good system can automatically provide links to it. While such complex systems are not readily available as yet, it is easy to see that reuse becomes more attractive.

To date, it is generally acknowledged that reuse of learning objects is not widespread. Some claim that there is not a large enough pool of LOs across all subjects and levels. Others claim that even if such repositories were available, the object assembly model of course development, where the instructor puts a course together by drawing objects from a range of repositories, is not a pedagogically sound or even an efficient approach. Interspersing LOs into an otherwise conventional (online) course may well be the dominant use in future. LOs then become just another teaching resource. This is a far cry from the initial promise of LOs, which was to take learning to new levels of personalisation and relevancy.

LIFELONG LEARNING

The European Union has defined 'lifelong learning' in a very broad way to include all types of learning at all ages:

- It is about acquiring and updating all kinds of abilities, interests, knowledge and qualifications from the pre-school years to post-retirement. It promotes the development of knowledge and competencies that will enable each citizen to adapt to the knowledge-based society and actively participate in all spheres of social and economic life, taking more control of his or her future;
- It is about valuing all forms of learning, including: formal learning, such as a degree course followed at university; non-formal learning, such as vocational skills acquired at the workplace; and informal learning, such as inter-generational learning – for example, where parents learn to use **ICT** through their children, or learning how to play an instrument together with friends. From the learner's point of view, therefore, lifelong learning is a continuous engagement in acquiring and applying knowledge and skills in the context of authentic, self-directed problems.

Several critical issues arise from this apparently simple statement about the nature of lifelong learning. These are:

- Learning should take place in the context of authentic, complex problems, rather than learning as answers to someone else's questions.
- Learning should be embedded in the pursuit of intrinsically reward-ing activities.
- Learning-on-demand needs to be supported because change is inevitable, it is impossible to cover any subject completely, and obsolescence is unavoidable.
- Organisational and **collaborative** learning recognise the essentially social nature of learning.
- Skills and processes that support learning as a lifetime habit must be developed.

These characteristics reflect very closely what we know about learn-ing. The first thing we know is that the learner is not a receptacle into which knowledge can be poured. Rather, learners construct their understanding uniquely and actively. This of course is quite at odds with the dominant instructional model of much formal education, which stresses additive content transmission. Second, learners develop different learning preferences, such that no one method of teaching will be equally effective for all learners. One way of coping effectively with this variation is to provide direct learning experiences so that each learner can engage with the subject in the way that is most suitable. We also know that learning occurs best in the context of a compelling problem – one that is specific and within the capacity of the learner to solve. In addition to this active engagement, learners need time for reflection. The challenge of solving problems produces a major surge in short-term neural activity. Building lasting cognitive connections, however, requires periods of reflective activity. Finally, effective learning needs a supportive social milieu and frequent opportunities for peer **interaction** and **feedback**. Consequently, both universities and schools need to move beyond seeing their mission as teaching facts and providing information, towards a much more challenging mission of teaching people how to learn and motivating them to do this throughout their lives.

Learning to learn has always been the Holy Grail of the education process and, as such, has always been more preached about than practised. The updated and arguably more urgently needed requirement now is the ability to elearn, that is, to learn using the facilities and **affordances** of the **online** environment. It is more urgent in that the need to learn facts and information has vastly reduced and the ability to find, manipulate, analyse, synthesise and re-purpose information has increased concomitantly. One of the key resources in developing these abilities is other people. Gone are the old threats that machines will replace teachers; machines can store, link and process information, but people transform it and add value to it. Tutors, mentors, **moderators** and online **facilitators** are now seen as the asset that makes all the difference to student **retention, motivation** and acceptance of elearning. Likewise, CBT (**computer-based training**) put up on the **web** with no human support is increasingly seen as unsuccessful and a 'horseless-carriage' use of connectivity. Because there is so much information available on the net, what is valued is knowing how to cope with it. Connecting with other people to share the load, to exchange tips and models for managing information, and to express ideas and give feedback, has become an essential element of elearning methodology. Fundamentally, this kind of learning rests on the understanding that the technology is *a* tool, not *the* tool.

The ability to use computers and other technology to improve learning, productivity and performance is a general definition of technology literacy. In fact, openness to new technologies and the willingness to try out new **software** and new communications opportunities are more important than expertise with a wide range of software. What we are witnessing in advanced Western countries is an upsurge in individuals realising the benefits of networked computing *themselves*, and through pursuing their own interests, hobbies and contacts, finding a whole new vehicle for effective learning – informally.

European policy makes a distinction between non-formal and informal learning based on the intention of the learner: informal learning results from activities in daily life at work, at home, at leisure; non-formal learning is intentional on the part of the learner and structured in terms of learning objectives, but is not accredited by a recognised education or training institution. In reality, most analysts admit that the boundaries between formal, non-formal and informal learning are blurred and can only be meaningfully drawn in relation to particular contexts. It is more useful to talk about dimensions of formality and to look at ways in which these aspects interrelate.

While online **communities** are being exploited by universities and schools, informal learning through online communities is a much larger phenomenon. Online communities can be categorised in a number of ways. One of these is:

- Geographic – defined by a physical location like a city or region;
- Demographic – defined by age, gender, race or nationality;
- Topical – defined by shared interest, like a fan club, hobby group or professional organisation;
- Activity-based – defined by a shared activity like shopping, investing, **gamification** or making music.

Arguably the most significant area of online community resulting in informal learning outcomes is the health sector. Informal learners who go online for health-related information want several things: to understand their problems better; to find information about diseases and treatments; to get support from others; to help fellow sufferers; to feel less afraid, and so on. Websites offer some information, but online communities are more personal resources.

Another example of informal learning is referred to as '**edutainment**', in the form of the plethora of semi-educational games which are available. The application of connected electronic games environments to 'real-life' educational events, including general election results, in-depth news coverage, online **simulations**, and military or medical training illustrate just some of the informal opportunities for learning not previously available. Online, informal opportunities to learn while playing are a phenomenon that cannot be ignored.

Gamification is changing the nature of learning and affecting attention spans; it demands multi-tasking and experiential and collaborative activity.

ICT is producing a major change in both the content and the processes of learning. Belonging to a range of **networks** is an informal strategy of increasing opportunities for lifelong learning. Professional updating courses offer another, more obvious opportunity. Self-initiated learning, using both online and offline resources, is a non-formal means of developing expertise in a chosen area.

LOGON/OFF OR LOGIN/OUT

This is the act of joining and/or leaving a computer system or a **network**, usually by typing a specific user identification (or 'user name') and a corresponding **password** known only to the individual user (and the system administrator.) Once a user has logged on to a computer system, the system will 'recognise' the individual user and accord them specific system privileges and constraints (e.g. students will gain access to approved student resources, but not to staff areas; students may be able to access the **internet**, or the **intranet**, and search certain **online libraries**). For this reason, it is important that when a user is finished working with the system s/he should log off as a user, otherwise the next person to use that computer could assume their online identity and gain access to personal files or restricted areas of the network.

LURKING

A derogatory term for people who read messages on **computer conferences** and/or **discussion boards** but do not contribute themselves. **Online** facilitators are always encouraging students to actively engage with the discussion, on the understanding that students will benefit from trying to express their thoughts and getting **feedback** on them from others. Nevertheless, lurking has been shown to be useful in some contexts and with some kinds of learners.

MENTORING

As part of the process of **distributed education**, and more generally in respect of elearning and the delivery of educational provision to learners who are at locations remote from their tutor, the appointment of a local staff contact, or mentor, is frequently encouraged. The mentor need not be an academic in the same field as the learner, and in fact may not currently be an active academic, as their main function is to provide generic support that is not necessarily discipline-based. A mentor will generally act as a point of local contact for a learner remote from the main campus, providing more than simply pastoral guidance, but not actually teaching or **tutoring** in the particular subject field of the learner. As such, a mentor will frequently provide a service for learners covering a range of disciplines (e.g. the various users of a local learning centre) or may be the appointed contact for the provision of **face-to-face** (**f2f**) guidance for a single class on a multi-campus institution where the tuition is being provided from another campus.

The mentor will commonly deal with very broad learning issues such as ensuring that learners are able to access their **MLE** from the learning centre, or that the **videoconference** connections are correctly established, and they may, for instance, invigilate for exams at appropriate times. Skills such as essay writing, correct citations for references and even basic diagnosis of literacy/numeracy deficiencies may be provided locally to learners by the mentor, who acts as a low-level academic support for the main tutorial team. Commonly the mentor will maintain close contacts with the student adviser for the course. The main function of the mentor is to support the system of distributed education by providing, as part of a wider team, general learner support and guidance that is also distributed around the **network**. Normally a mentor would not be considered a part of the core academic team but rather is an integral member of the learner support services that are so crucial to the creation of a sense of learning **community** amongst distributed learners, which in turn promotes better learner engagement, **interaction** and course **retention**.

META TAG

The meta tag is used by search engines to allow them to more accurately list a site in their indexes. Meta tags are descriptive words in a website code which help search engines identify the main topics of a website.

METADATA

This is the term for information about a **learning object** that enables it to be stored and retrieved from a **database**. It is information about the learning object, not information in the learning object. In short, it is data about the data. Learning object metadata (LOM) provides information about the attributes and format of the learning object, such as title, author, date, educational context and intent. Both **meta tags** and metadata are essential to control work flow and output of information from the repository.

MICRO-BLOGGING

A form of **blogging**, which utilises short **posts** (text, images or video) which are often sent frequently to a communications network. Typically, these posts can be linked to a **web feed** to enable regular updating of information, and they can be used to facilitate **collaborative learning/work** and access to **mobile learning**.

MICRO-CREDENTIALING

Micro-credentials are certifications for evidencing achievement or accomplishment in relation to a specific topic, skill or aspect of practice. Micro-credentials can take the form of nano-degrees, digital certificates and **digital badges** which are issued by the group or organisation who are offering the learning or training experience in question. Micro-credentials are valuable for evidencing to employers or educational institutions that specific knowledge or skillsets have been developed, and for the individual to also allow them to evidence active engagement in their own ongoing vocational and professional development.

MLE

An MLE is a managed learning environment (see **VLE**).

MOBILE LEARNING

Mobile learning is any form of learning utilising digital resources enabling **accessibility** of the **internet** from portable devices while the user is on the move, including from a **laptop** or **tablet**, and increasingly from a **smartphone** and **e-book** reader.

MODEM

This word has come to signify a device connected to a computer that modulates and demodulates the digital data produced by a computer and encodes this as analogue data for transfer through an ordinary telephone line, to be decoded at the other end into digital data and read by another computer system. The modem was a necessary device to allow dial-up **email** and any **internet** connection before the arrival of digital telephone lines and **broadband** access to the internet. Although still common, their use is likely to become redundant for normal connections as digital connections become more commonplace, though there may still be a use for them in certain specialised situations such as separating multiple signals in wireless transmissions and in making use of domestic power lines to also carry broadband internet data.

MODERATOR

Sometimes called 'emoderator', the moderator is a person who presides over **online** conferences and **discussion boards**. In the context of elearning, the moderator is usually the tutor. The primary function of the moderator is facilitating the online discussions. This means any or all of the following:

1.   Choosing the topic for discussion.
2.   **Posting** questions strategically to keep the discussion going.
3.   Encouraging **interactivity** with students in the topic through adding background information sharing relevant anecdotes.

4. Modelling the kind of responses expected from students, especially synthesising and summarising messages.
5. Pointing to outside resources, **URLs**, articles or books as sources of information on the topic.
6. Sending **emails** to students privately if they are contributing too much or not enough.
7. Acknowledging good inputs from students.
8. Weaving together discussion threads and summarising at the end of the discussion.

The moderator may have a number of administrative duties, such as setting up new discussion areas, and technical duties, such as answering IT queries and/or **assessment** responsibilities. The role is usually heaviest at the beginning of the course when students need a lot of support and confidence-building, and the moderator needs to set the tone of the discussions. Turn-taking is an important skill to encourage in the group, as is the ability to express opinions without being over-bearing. The job has often been likened to a good host of a party.

MODULE

This is a short, structured part of a course of academic study. There is a great deal of variation from one educational provider to another in the size or length of a module. In general terms, there has been a tendency in recent years to divide the academic year more flexibly into a number of related units or blocks (or modules) of related study topics. Some educational providers allow learners to choose to study modules independently as free-standing short courses. A typical module might last for the duration of one semester, or term, and would necessitate 100–150 hours of study, possibly by means of **distributed education** or other study modes that provide a level of flexibility for learners. A number of modules on related themes can be grouped together (by the institution and/or the learner) to form a recognised course of study, leading to the achievement of an academic award. This building block of the module has the advantage that learners can combine a few modules together for an award, or progress to collecting a few more modules for a higher award, and so on. Each module is on a discrete academic topic and may be assessed independently of any other modules.

MOOC (MASSIVE OPEN ONLINE COURSE)

A MOOC is an open **online** course, delivered through the **web** and associated technologies, that is free to enrol on and which is designed to accommodate very large numbers of geographically dispersed online learners. MOOCs typically support learning through providing **access** to course materials (including, for example, new or repurposed recorded lectures, videos and study guides) alongside opportunities for participants to learn through online dialogue and discussion with each other, and to complete specific individual or collaborative tasks and activities.

The first MOOC is widely acknowledged to have been the 'Connectivism and Connective Knowledge' open online course first offered in 2008, and the subsequent growth of MOOCs through the several thousand that have been offered worldwide since then has seen the MOOC ethos and basic model become a central part of the burgeoning **open education** movement. Diversification in the MOOC model has led to a general distinction between cMOOCs and xMOOCs. The former are based on the principles of **connectivism**, and are primarily about connected learning and knowledge building. The latter, xMOOCs, tend to have a more structured syllabus. They are more instructor- than participant-focused, and there is usually a specific purpose for completing the course (e.g. to evidence successful learning of the syllabus, and/or to enable potential progression into a formal programme of study).

Various **platforms** now exist through which universities, consortia of universities and other providers are offering access to MOOCs in their various forms, both to support informal open online learning and also to offer certification or accreditation that can lead or contribute towards undertaking formal programmes of study. At the time of writing, leading MOOC platforms include Coursera, FutureLearn, Udacity, Udemy, EdX and OERu.

MOOCs have been criticised for not fulfilling their early promise of widening access to and participation in higher education opportunities for those who are seeking them, with several studies in the sector having shown that the vast majority of participants in MOOCs already have higher education qualifications and are based in the Global North (Johnston et al., 2019).

However, as MOOCs continue to mature it is becoming apparent that they offer substantial educational opportunities in relation to **lifelong learning**, ensuring currency of knowledge in participants' areas of expertise or related areas of practice and expertise, and for facilitating progression to further formal educational opportunities for those able to meet the requirements for completing MOOCs that offer either course credits or credentialing.

MOTIVATION

The disposition and commitment of the learner to learn, motivation, is considered to be the most important factor influencing learning effectiveness. Motivation to learn may be defined as those factors that energise and direct behavioural patterns organised around a learning goal. There are two sets of factors which are included in the notion of motivation: extrinsic and intrinsic factors. Extrinsic factors originate in external structures and reward; for example, pay, professional standards, organisational policies and norms, as well as requirements originating in formal learning programmes where the individual is enrolled. Intrinsic factors stem from inner or self-driven pressures to grow and achieve, and thus include personal desires, the need to conform, the quest for esteem, and challenges such as solving problems or supporting others. In terms of elearning, research has shown that intrinsically motivated participants are relatively more explorative and do qualitatively different things **online**. This finding has been confirmed through students' self-reported inclination to explore the environment.

MULTIMEDIA

'Multimedia' is a term that is often used very loosely and therefore has decreasing academic value. In general, it is used to describe the bringing together of a variety of different media to create a rich learning environment; for example, **webpages** with **audio/video clips** embedded, accompanied by printed learning resources and an **email** or **audioconference** link. The progressive **convergence** of digital devices, such as computers, personal digital assistants (PDAs) and mobile telephones, has allowed a greater scope and diversity of multimedia opportunities for education, and to some extent has reduced its novelty.

MULTIPLE CHOICE QUESTION (MCQ)

This is a form of **assessment** in which the learner is presented with a statement or question, and a number of different responses, only one of which is correct, with the other 'answers' being plausible but incorrect (distractors). MCQs are a form of objective test, that is, they are designed to enable the marker to assess the knowledge of the learner without exercising any subjective judgement on its value. Although they have been criticised by some educationalists for only assessing a superficial level of knowledge, MCQs are frequently included in the **course design** of elearning **modules** as self-test or formative assessments to allow the learner to evaluate his/her understanding of the topic and measure progress. The inclusion of MCQs on more sophisticated **VLEs** or **MLEs** allows the tutor to not simply provide a yes/no response but to give immediate **feedback** to the learner. This feedback may be in the form of an explanation for the incorrect choice, or it may provide deeper layers of information to more fully explain the reason for the correct or incorrect choice (e.g. a **hyperlink** to another **webpage** with detailed **case studies**, or to an academic article on the topic in an **online library**). Although well designed MCQs require time and skill to construct, they have the advantage that they then function automatically (without tutor intervention) and are suitable for **asynchronous learning** and **distributed education** activities. Some complex MCQs will allow for the random selection of questions from a 'question bank', and will adjust the level of questions presented to the learner in relation to their level of performance (i.e. presenting harder questions if the learner seems to be finding them too easy, or providing easier questions when the learner continually fails to make the correct choice).

The facilities of the **web** have allowed MCQ developers to use **multimedia** and a wide variety of question types. For example:

- True/false questions;
- Assertion-reason questions (combining elements of MCQ and true/false);
- Multiple-response questions (involving the selection of more than one answer from a list and picking from a list of options x, y, z, etc.);
- Text/numerical questions (involving the input of text or numbers at the keyboard);
- Ranking questions (requiring students to relate items in a column to one another, thus testing the knowledge of the order of events);

- Sequencing questions (requiring the student to position text in a given sequence, which is particularly good for testing methodology).

NETIQUETTE

A common term for 'network etiquette' or the 'rules of engagement' for **online** practitioners. Due to the brief and sometimes terse nature of **email** and messages to **discussion boards** or other **computer conferencing** applications, it is very easy to offend other users unintentionally. On some occasions giving offence may lead to **flaming** while more generally it will simply discourage **interaction** between learners and a lessening of **trust** in the members of online **communities**. Netiquette is a response aimed at minimising these negative aspects by providing at the outset a clear set of guidelines on how online users should show consideration for each other. Simple indications of the tone of the message, or the intention of the user, can be given by the incorporation of **emoticons** in the text to suggest humour, irony, etc. or by indicating emphasis by SHOUTING in capitals to stress KEY words.

More generally, as in other areas of life, it is helpful to imagine yourself in the shoes of the other person. If offence is accidentally caused by a message that is misinterpreted, users should not be slow to apologise and correct the error. Generally speaking, regular online users are pretty tolerant of short, to-the-point messages and bad spelling, but they will be less tolerant if they are required to waste time with irrelevant email, repetitive bad manners, or actions that cause them to lose performance on their computer (such as sending complex files or large images). Etiquette includes simple rules such as: don't copy an embarrassing message to a third party without the consent of the original sender; avoid using offensive, rude, or racist language; and try to avoid inconveniencing other users by, for example, attaching large files that **modem** users will find slow or impossible to **download**.

Take care not to clog up users' email accounts by distributing unwanted messages as a result of 'copying to all' rather than simply copying to the person who was intended, and basically show a little common courtesy to other online users. As a rule, CMCs afford a user opportunities to read other users' messages, pause, reflect offline, and then return online to **post** a reply that is carefully considered and appropriate. Breaches of netiquette most frequently occur when users give rapid-fire responses to online comments that they later regret when they have had time to cool down. Good elearning courses normally devote some induction time at the start of the course to issues of netiquette, procedures for communicating with tutors and general online protocol.

NETWORKS

The ability to join two or more computer systems together to exchange information has led to the establishment of various types of computer networks, including the **LAN**, the WAN and, ultimately, the **internet** through which many of these networks are globally linked. With respect to elearning, the terms 'network learning' and 'network courses' have arisen from the ability to link geographically scattered learners together in one 'class' to benefit from techniques of **distributed education**. Networks can function for either **synchronous** or **asynchronous learning**, depending upon the **software** applications being used and the educational purpose of the connection. The **peer-to-peer** connections can be used for student support, as well as **collaborative work**, and as a means of facilitating educational **interaction** amongst the members of the network.

ONLINE

Being online is the activity of being engaged in using a computer **network**, such as the **internet** or an **intranet**, for sending/receiving **email**, using a **browser** to search the **web**, and/or for transferring files from one computer to another. To get online, the user is normally required to **logon** with a unique user identification and self-selected **password**, then select a **software** application to connect to the relevant network. The fact that so much **interaction** can take place during this networked activity has given rise to the word 'online' being used extensively as a descriptive prefix for many other activities and concepts, such as 'online learning' as a synonym for elearning, 'online personality' for the **avatar** or the characteristic personal traits that the user chooses to display while networking, or '**online libraries**' for the literature, images and other resources that are available over the internet. In contrast, 'offline' is frequently used to describe work or activities that are prepared in advance when the user is not online, then **uploaded**, or transferred to another location by 'cutting-and-pasting' or as an **attachment** during an online connection, rather than spending time (and money) typing long messages 'live' while online.

ONLINE LIBRARIES

This is developing as a generic term for **online** access to a range of library resources and is becoming a key component of **blended learning** approaches to higher education. Sometimes called 'hybrid libraries', the initial concept was to have online access to the catalogue of a distant library, but this has expanded rapidly with the availability of digital resources and online journals. Allied to the concept of **lifelong learning**, in which people are encouraged to participate in **flexible learning** throughout their lives, online libraries are growing in popularity as a partial solution to encouraging **accessibility** to appropriate learning resources. This is closely allied to **distributed learning**, whereby education can be delivered to individuals and **communities** wherever they are located. As elearning has encouraged the spread of learners in off-campus sites, of necessity the need has grown to provide adequate library resources on an equitable basis to students who may be many miles (or hours) away from a conventional paper-based academic library.

Online libraries now include gateway sites (portals) that provide a single link to a list, sometimes searchable, of other identified useful sources of information. These lists may link to another **webpage**, or an online academic journal through commercial services such as BIDS, Infotrac, or EBSCO providing abstracts and/or full-text articles. Increasingly, as with 'conventional libraries', the online library may contain links to sources of digital images, sound files (e.g. guidance commentary or interviews), **video clips**, e-books, data sets and other forms of digitally stored materials. In some specific subject areas, librarians and course tutors may have gathered together selected resources on a subject, such as by **digitizing** articles from journals or chapters from books under a **copyright** licence agreement. As more material is being made available digitally to access over the **internet**, some observers have suggested that the **digital divide** of the future will not just be between those people who do and do not have access to the internet but, in reality, between those who are and are not e-literate, that is, able to search, identify, select and reuse digital information from elibraries and other online repositories.

An increasing number of university and college libraries provide orientation guides for their learners in the form of subject guides to online resources accessible through their own institutional webpages. Under such systems, course teams can build up sets of digital resources that can be carefully tailored to the needs of learners on specific courses and/or **modules** of courses with copyright clearance for a certain number of learners and duration. Key benefits of this system are in being able to provide quality materials directly to the desk of learners, particularly learners in rural, remote and/or international locations; the repository is easily maintained and quickly updated, and can include copies of rare and fragile documents, or materials now out of print. With the addition of sound and image files it is possible to customise a **multimedia** range of resources to enhance the learning experience, and this can be provided at various levels of depth for each individual subject, e.g. as backup notes for a session in a module, or more detailed resources for learners who want to go into more depth, or even as a specialist option for higher level students and researchers.

OPEN ACCESS

This is a term which is usually applied to sources of digital information which are available on the **web**, or through an **internet** connection, which are freely available (no charge) and do not require special rights or **software** in order to access the resource. Typical examples might be images which are available on the **Creative Commons**, or videos on **YouTube**. There is a big drive in **open education** to embrace the concept of **open publishing**, to give easy access to academic journals which are free to view and share, as well as **open textbooks** and other learning materials such as **learning objects** and **online** courses (in part or in their entirety). **Open educational resources** are, by definition, open access materials which have been made available to assist learning.

OPEN DATA

The idea and practice of making data freely and openly available for distribution, use and reuse by anyone. This could include openly licensed, **open access** governmental data, scientific data, environmental data and data relating to public services, as well as data sets pertaining to culture and heritage. Within education, one increasingly common use of open data relates to open publishing of research data sets for reuse by other researchers, including students, for their own projects and purposes.

OPEN EDUCATIONAL PRACTICE

Distinct from **open learning** as we have defined it, although related to the ethos associated with open learning, the term 'open educational practice' is a more recent one which was first used to refer in general to the use of **open educational resources** (OER) in learning and teaching. Currently, the term 'open educational practice' is a multifaceted one which captures the philosophy and practice of democratising access to education and educational opportunities through the development, sharing and use of OER, the provision of open online learning opportunities through, for example, **MOOCs**, and through **open textbooks** and open **digital scholarship**. There is also a growing understanding of, and commitment to, forms of open educational practice that encompass and interest open online, open 'on campus' and open 'in the community' forms of open educational practice (e.g. Johnston et al., 2019).

See also: **open educational resources; open access; Creative Commons; COOC.**

OPEN EDUCATIONAL RESOURCES (OER)

Open educational resources are freely available and openly licensed digital materials, media and resources which are made available for use or adapted use in learning and teaching. OER can comprise specific individual digital objects for learning such as an image, video, an interactive self-test or a piece of text, in addition to sets of resources relating to a particular topics, **open textbooks**, and entire courses that are openly licensed and available for **reusing, reworking and remixing**.

There are now countless numbers of OER collections and directories relating to almost any subject or disciplinary area of study that you can imagine, and we point towards where you can find some of these in the Further Resources section.

See also: **open educational practice; Creative Commons**

OPEN LEARNING

Open learning is a philosophy of education that values more opportunity for learners to engage in various ways with the educational process, not just through **face-to-face (f2f)** interaction. The term is used most commonly in the UK. In Australia, the equivalent is referred to as **'flexible learning'**. Some commentators claim that there is no one definition of open learning; rather, there are a range of elements which could be included in a definition. For example:

- Location – students and teacher may be in different locations;
- Time – **interaction** can be in real time or more likely **asynchronous**;
- Entry qualifications – usually less stringent than for campus universities;
- Technology – a range of media may be used to support the delivery of the course, from large-scale industrialised processes to small-group teaching;
- Communication – can be face-to-face or more likely technology-mediated. Alternatively, it can be a mixture of both.

The educational philosophy of open learning is usually learner-centred, and the educational institution attempts to remove barriers that impede access to traditional courses. Usually, institutions offer choice over some of the following:

- medium or media, whether print, online, television or video;
- place of study, whether at home, in the workplace or on campus;
- pace of study, whether closely paced or unstructured;

- support mechanisms, whether tutors on demand, **audioconferences** or computer-assisted learning; and
- entry and exit points.

In short, educational provision can be called open learning according to the degree to which the institution is course-centred or learner-centred, and to the degree of flexibility existing in the areas such as admission policies, examination requirements, curriculum modifications and delivery methods.

OPEN SOURCE

This refers to **software** that has a freely available source code (the programming language) which is available to the public at no cost. The software should be distributed freely and include all relevant documentation. Programmers are able to rewrite and improve on the software but are normally expected to return their improvements into the public domain at no charge. Some educational establishments have moved towards using open source software as the **platform** to operate their virtual learning environment (**VLE**) (or more correctly, managed learning environment – **MLE**) on the grounds that they can avoid paying commercial licence fees to the suppliers and are better able to customise the MLE to their specific requirements. On the other hand, not having a supplier to maintain the MLE means that the institution itself must incur the costs of running and developing their platform. In some cases, although the software itself is distributed at no cost, some companies offer commercial services to install and maintain the system on behalf of an institution. Advantages of using open source materials include the ability to select and change the appearance and functionality of the MLE and the ability to have a major influence on the future design of the system. This may be a major consideration, for example, when customising the VLE or MLE to allow for working in a minority language. A well-known example of an open source VLE is Moodle.

OPEN TEXTBOOK

An open textbook is a textbook that has been published and is distributable under an open license (e.g. a **Creative Commons** or other form of open license) and is freely available online for use by teachers, learners and the wider public. Open textbooks are commonly published as **e-textbooks** and **downloadable** digital documents, and sometimes also in audio form.

Within the field of **open education**, and more widely in the education sector, there is a growing discourse around open textbooks as a social justice, both in relation to providing a more affordable education for college and university students, and also in relation to the sharing of knowledge as a public good. Within the US, the Open Textbook Network (OTN) is one of several consortia or initiatives that are active in promoting the development, distribution and use of open textbooks in higher education (https://research.cehd.umn.edu/otn/), while the @UKOpenTextbooks project is undertaking a similar mission within the UK national context (http://ukopentextbooks.org/).

PASSWORD

A unique identifying combination of letters, numbers and/or symbols that is used in combination with a specific user name to identify an individual person and allow them access to secure sections of the **internet**. Passwords are commonly used to enable learners to enter **MLEs** (or **VLEs**) and **chatrooms**, as well as to send **email** and **instant messaging** communications.

PDF

The abbreviation for 'portable document format' that describes a file format developed by the **software** company Adobe Systems to create and save documents that can be transferred across **networks** to other computers. The value of a PDF file is that it can be viewed in the style of the original document, regardless of the software or **hardware** used by either the sender or receiver. A PDF file may contain text and/or **graphics**, and may be very simple or very complex, but the formatting retains the original look of the documents. A number of readers are available for different operating systems and can be **downloaded** free over the **internet**.

PEDAGOGY

The term 'pedagogy' is commonly used to refer to the theory and practice of education, with the term 'pedagogic research' often used to refer to research undertaken into dimensions of the theory and practice of learning, teaching and **assessment**, or cognitive aspects of how learning occurs. However, the literal translation of 'pedagogy' from the Greek language is 'leading children', and some references to pedagogy in the educational literature specifically relate to learning and teaching in relation to young people. '**Andragogy**' is the preferred term for some theorists and practitioners to refer to the theory and practice of adult education, while the term '**heutagogy**' has a distinct meaning in relation to self-determined learning.

PEER ASSESSMENT

The process of a learner marking an **assessment** of another learner, for the purposes of **feedback** and/or as a contribution to the final grade, is known as peer assessment. Peer assessment is also used amongst academic staff members to comment on the work of other staff colleagues. Peer assessment may be formative (for the purposes of ongoing improvement) or summative (for a final grade). It has the benefit that, in addition to the normal value of gaining feedback on the quality of submitted work, the person who is marking the work gains experience in assessing the critical points in the work of someone at their own level, thereby becoming more critically aware of the subject matter. Peer assessment has been used in elearning as a means of prompting **interaction** amongst learners, often using a **VLE** and/or a **discussion board** in order to share the comments with other learners and involve them more fully in the process of understanding what is meant by quality work at the appropriate level. Peer assessment can be regarded as a form of **peer-to-peer** learning and/or **collaborative work** that is structured around an academic **module** or course. In attempting to incorporate peer assessment as a formal part of elearning, it will be necessary to clearly define in advance the specific nature/aims of the assessment, the marking scheme by which merit is awarded, and the criteria for pass or fail, etc. These definitions need to be shared with both the examined and the examiners, and this process in itself can be utilised as a beneficial learning activity for all learners in benchmarking elements of **quality assurance**.

PEER-TO-PEER

A reference to the **interaction** between learners for mutual learning and support (or indeed between staff members in a form of supportive **collaborative work**). The adoption of **constructivism** as a **pedagogy** for elearning encourages learners to build upon their experiences in order to put their learning into context. The ability to **network** learners in a **VLE** or **MLE** allows learners to share their experiences and to learn from each other as well as from the course tutor. Some of the more imaginative forms of academic **assessment** include peer-to-peer monitoring and marking of work done by other students, including written assignments, presentations and/or project work. Peer-to-peer support and collaborative working lends itself very well to a diversity of communication media (e.g. **videoconference, email, discussion boards**, etc.) and is ideally suited for **distributed education**.

PERSONAL LEARNING ENVIRONMENT (PLE)

There are various definitions of the term 'personal learning environment' (PLE), reflecting different views of what a PLE actually constitutes. Within the context of digital education, Saadatmand and Kumpulainen (2013, p.70) offer a helpful definition of 'personal learning environment' as '... a combination of social media-enabled systems, applications, and services which help learners to take control of their learning by aggregating, manipulating, and creating digital contents and learning artefacts, and sharing them with others'.

See also: **personal learning network, content aggregation, Domain of One's Own**

PERSONAL LEARNING NETWORK (PLN)

Related to but arguably distinct from a **personal learning environment**, a personal learning network comprises the **network** of individuals and groups that an individual follows, connects with or to, or engages in dialogue with in order to develop and share their own knowledge within a particular subject, discipline or area of practice. A PLN is not limited to interactions within the digital domain, but the development by the individual of their own digital network of contacts and connections is a key aspect of a PLN.

Some definitions of 'personal learning environment' include PLNs as a feature of PLEs.

PLAGIARISM

The act of plagiarism occurs when a person passes off the words or ideas of another person as their own. The fault lies not in the use of the words or ideas but in presenting them as something new and original, rather than derived from an existing source. Institutions vary in the seriousness with which they deal with plagiarism: some consider it theft and police students' work through surveillance and plagiarism detection **software**. An alternative approach is to combine smart assignment design with teaching students what plagiarism is, how to reference sources and why academic honesty matters.

The reason that plagiarism has risen to prominence as a major academic problem is partly that plagiarism has become so easy with the proliferation of **internet** sites and partly that the distinction between publicly and privately owned information has blurred. The concept of ownership of physical property is well established. The notion of intellectual property is not nearly so well accepted. People who would never consider stealing records or tapes from a music shop often do not have the same compunction about **peer-to-peer** file sharing of music. Furthermore, the seemingly public nature of so much **online** content masks the true ownership issues. Electronic resources are so easily reproduced that there exists a collective amnesia about intellectual property rights over internet material.

Students who might have reservations about copying words and ideas from a book without acknowledgement are less concerned about doing the same from internet sites.

The problem has been exacerbated by the growth of online paper mills that exist solely for the purpose of providing students with essays and homework solutions. Students may select from large **databases** of essays and solutions or they may pay to have something customised for their particular use. There are hundreds of such sites on the internet and many are profitable ventures.

For students working in a second language, the excuse is that 'the original author explained it so much better than they could'. Turning something that is well written into faltering language seems to them a foolish and retrograde step.

At a more general level, students often ask, 'How can words and ideas be stolen? Surely we are all reusing others' ideas all the time'. With the rise of interest in **learning objects** and re-versioning course content, there is a movement away from instructors writing new material from scratch. It is doubly ironic therefore that academics are being encouraged to reuse content but students are condemned for it! The fact is that legally, it is still considered plagiarism even when the ideas have been put into different words. If the original source of the ideas is not acknowledged, it is plagiarism.

Teachers are now being encouraged to take positive action to prevent plagiarism by integrating discussion about it into seminars, by creating assignments that discourage plagiarism and encourage original thinking, and by pointing to different types of plagiarism; in particular, plagiarism from the internet. The internet has various guidelines for students on how to avoid unintentional plagiarism, tips on how to cite references correctly, and suggestions for developing good research and writing skills.

There are many gradations of plagiarism, from quoting a source too closely without citing that source, through to blatantly presenting the words of another as if they were your own original words.

There are several things that teachers can do to prevent plagiarism:

1   In larger classes, teachers might insist on a research trail which becomes part of the submitted paper. Or they could demand a research plan which makes use of the library. Alternatively, they could ask for all the original handwritten notes, marked

photocopies or printouts, and copies of all computer disk files. The research plan and the student's use of them could be a formal part of the project.

2   In small classes, the research process should be part of the assignment and made available to others in the group. Students can be asked to comment on each other's research proposals. These occasions can be a major learning opportunity as workable and unworkable proposals are discussed, as well as interesting and trite ones.

Most plagiarism detection software is designed to detect material cut and pasted from the internet. For large classes, there is software that detects identical or very similar submissions. Some software will compile databases of submissions so that new work can be compared with earlier work. The threat of using plagiarism detection software is often enough to deter students.

PLATFORM

The term 'platform' in elearning refers to the framework of **hardware** and/or **software** that enables a computer to run and interact with users. Usually this means the type of operating system of the computer **network**, though it is sometimes (erroneously) used to refer to the framework of the **VLE** architecture with which users interact. Quite simply, the platform is synonymous with the computer operating system that enables users to host other forms of computer software.

PODCAST

A form of digital audio resource which is made available on the **internet**, that users can **download** to listen to on their computer or mobile device (e.g. a **smartphone**). Typically, a podcast will be part of a series on a theme, which users can subscribe to using RSS or an alert system when new podcasts become available.

POST OR POSTING

Members of online **communities** can send an electronic message to other members of their community by sending the equivalent of an **email** to a common **discussion board**, and this message appears on the discussion board as a posting. Students would therefore be encouraged to post their comments on a particular topic for further discussion, usually by sending short electronic messages, but perhaps also by including an **attachment** with some large piece of the students' work for comment or for **assessment**. Successive postings build up over a period of time as an **asynchronous** discussion on the course work by a group of learners who perhaps never meet **face-to-face** (**f2f**) due to the fact that they are separated by distance or time constraints.

PROBLEM-BASED LEARNING (PBL)

This is a learner-centred educational method that challenges students to 'learn to learn', working either individually or cooperatively in groups to seek solutions to real-world problems. These problems are used to engage students' curiosity and motivate them to learn the subject matter. PBL prepares students to think critically and analytically, and to find and use appropriate learning resources. PBL aims to produce independent learners who can continue to learn on their own in life and in their chosen careers. The responsibility of the teacher in PBL is to provide the educational materials and guidance that facilitate learning. PBL is based on real-world problems which are often messy and complex, and are aimed at ensuring recall and application to future problems. The PBL process is **learner-centred** at every step. Learning through exploring problem situations is not unique to elearning; in fact, problem-based learning was popularised in the 1960s as a result of research with medical students at McMaster University in Canada. The research stemmed from a desire to develop in medical students the ability to relate the knowledge they had learned to the problems presented by patients, something that few medical students could do well.

What the research highlighted was a clear difference between problem-solving and problem-based learning. In the latter, problem scenarios are used to encourage students to engage themselves in the learning process; PBL is an educational format that is centred around the discussion and learning that emanates from a clinically based problem. It is a method that encourages independent learning and gives students practice in tackling puzzling situations and defining their own gaps in understanding in the context of relevant clinical problems, hopefully making it more likely that they will be able to recall the material later in the clinical setting. It is a way of learning that encourages a deeper understanding of the material rather than superficial coverage.

Yet the attraction of problem-based learning and its uptake in the 1970s and 1980s in Canada, Australia and the US, and in the late 1980s in the UK, seemed to be not only its timely emergence in relation to other worldwide changes in higher education but also because of new debates about professional education. These related to a growing recognition that there needed to be not just a different view of learning and professional education but also a different view about relationships between industry and education, between learning and society, and between government and universities. Problem-based learning has been a huge area of growth in the UK, particularly in the last five years, and as yet there has been relatively little provision of resources to support its implementation, development and research.

QR CODES

Originally standing for 'quick response code', QR marks are a form of two-dimensional barcode containing data which can be read optically to supply additional information such as CVs, documents and links to a **webpage**. They are often used on posters, etc., where space is limited.

QUALITY ASSURANCE

Questions about quality in elearning are constantly being raised and yet there is little agreement about what constitutes high quality. This is because 'fitness for purpose' is the ultimate determinant of quality. What is an outstandingly good course in one context is unsuccessful in another because the whole learning situation is different. Quality is one of those things that is hard to define but 'you know it when you see it'. The term 'quality assurance' usually has overtones of checking and evaluating to determine compliance with specific requirements or learning outcomes. The term 'quality enhancement' is what is considered when, for example, a programme previously taught **face-to-face (f2f)** is transformed for the **online** environment.

A number of quality assurance guidelines have been developed for elearning, some derived from campus teaching, others developed specifically for the online environment. The areas covered in such guidelines are usually similar: **course design** and **tutoring** processes, student services, technology and course delivery processes.

Course design and tutoring

Benchmarks of quality for course design focus on the stated learning outcomes and the way in which the course content flows from these. Similarly, the **assessment** processes should reflect all of the learning outcomes offering students opportunities to demonstrate their level of mastery of each one. The quality of online **tutoring** is critical to students achieving the learning outcomes. Requirements of high-quality online tutors include the obvious ones such as depth of knowledge of the subject area, and presentation and organisational skills. In addition, the interest, willingness and ability to interact with students online and to provide **feedback** and guidance are vital attributes. The quality of **interaction** with the tutor is one of the key indicators in many student surveys about elearning.

Student services

This domain can be subdivided into the services needed before registration, support during the learning experience, and the continued connection between learners and the institution after the particular course or programme has been completed. Access to support materials (e.g. on how to be an elearner or how to use the elearning **platform** or **online libraries**) should be developed as generic university services.

Technology

The **platform** for the delivery of elearning, for both the course content and the interactions, must provide security and privacy of data and communication as a basic minimum. Prior notice of the downtime for maintenance is an important consideration, as are the processes and personnel needed to handle unanticipated technical problems. A telephone **helpdesk** to answer students' queries and an online conference and set of **FAQs** for common problems are all facilities of high-quality elearning provision. The extent to which administrative processes such as registration, monitoring, counselling or complaints are handled online will depend on the individual educational institution. An online system for submission of assignments is one platform component that is an important feature of elearning provision.

Course delivery processes

Robust systems for handling a range of course delivery issues are required when teaching takes place online rather than face-to-face. Student handbooks, course guides and a course calendar need to be prepared and put online before the students **log on**. Library resources need to be identified, **copyright** cleared if necessary, and the materials made available online. Monitoring processes need to be agreed and implemented. Elearning is 'front-loaded' in terms of time, just as **distance learning** is; the need for preparation and planning are crucial to both.

Quality assurance processes are often imposed by bodies external to the university, and compliance can therefore be given grudgingly. However, when staff negotiate their own standards, the quality of elearning programmes is usually higher. Furthermore, compliance is self-sustaining without enforcement or policing.

The problem of **plagiarism** in elearning programmes has an impact on quality. Plagiarism is not a problem unique to elearning, but it is certainly exacerbated by the ease with which material from the **web** can be cut and pasted into an essay and passed off as original work by the student. Furthermore, whole essays can be bought online and websites offering to tailor material for specific essay topics can easily be found.

Plagiarism detection **software** has been developed to cope with the problem, and student guidelines have been developed to increase awareness and understanding about plagiarism. Re-designing assessments to tie them in to the online discussions, and to include a succession of drafts or outlines, is more effective and can lead to better-quality work from students.

Evaluation of the learning provision by the educational institution is as essential for elearning as it is for face-to-face teaching. Developing web-based questionnaires is the obvious procedure on elearning programmes. As always with programme evaluation measures and processes, it is critical to build these into the programme design from the beginning.

Examples of elearning quality assurance guidelines are those developed by The Quality Assurance Agency of the UK for distance education, which are applicable to elearning as well. An Australian framework has also been developed (see www.qaa.ac.uk). Most higher education institutions have quality assurance processes for learning and, if they teach online, these have been adapted or rewritten.

RETENTION

This term describes the ability to retain learners over the course of a **module** of study, rather than having them drop out as a result of any difficulties that they might experience. Due to the fact that elearning enables students to pursue their studies in a solitary environment, rather isolated from other students, concern has been expressed that often their problems remain undetected until it is too late and they withdraw from the course. There is very little hard evidence in the academic literature that the retention rate for elearners is either better or worse than other forms of **distance learning**, but where the **motivation** of elearners is strong, the additional flexibility is frequently perceived as an advantage. The main problem stems from the fact that in most elearning situations, the learners are at locations remote from the tutor, who is not therefore in a position to spot learner difficulties as s/he might do in a classroom situation. For this reason, many educationalists have developed a variety of ways to encourage **interaction** between learners and to foster participation in **tutor groups** that allow early identification of developing problems. Regular formative **assessment** to give constructive **feedback** to learners on their academic progress, together with a range of **online** support resources, (such as tips on how to write a good essay, how to reference properly, etc.) have been used to assist learners to feel more comfortable with the more individualistic demands of elearning.

It is common for universities that make significant use of elearning to allocate a student adviser to each course, with the aim of providing a level of personal support for students that is not directly linked to the learner's tutor (and therefore to any learning problems associated with the teaching style of that tutor).

REUSING, REWORKING AND REMIXING

Reusing, reworking and remixing are sometimes referred to as the 'three R's' of working with **open education resources**, although guidelines also exist relating to the reusing, reworking and remixing of copyrighted material for educational purposes.

In short, in relation to OER, reusing is the reuse of an openly licensed education resource in original form and format, although not necessarily for the same educational context, purpose or activity for which it was originally designed. Reworking involves adapting an existing OER, through removing or adding content and elements, to better contextualise it to the new use for which it is intended. Remixing is the process of adapting and reworking a range of OER, often with added original content, to create something new.

In all forms of working with OER, whether reusing, reworking or remixing, the original OER source materials and resources should be acknowledged. When producing a reworked or remixed OER that was made available for use through a **Creative Commons** license, the corresponding license should be used on the reworked or remixed OER.

ROLE PLAY

A form of educational **interaction** and **peer-to-peer** communication between learners in which the participants take on the role(s) of characters other than themselves. In **gamification** and **serious games**, this may take the form of an **avatar** as a representation of the participant, who controls the movement of that character in the **online** environment. It has been employed extensively both in online and in offline educational contexts, particularly with reference to **problem–based learning** (**PBL**) and vocational learning/training situations. In elearning, it is common to use a **discussion board** and assign roles to students to facilitate a learning activity, such as chair a meeting, present an alternative point of view (with supporting evidence), or summarise and propose action points, in order to demonstrate that students are fully conversant with a particular subject. A key point is usually that the role is more important than the result of the role-playing and is used to provide a means for learners to gain experience in playing different roles, e.g. being 'for' or 'against' in a debate, even though the participant may personally hold contrary views.

RSS

'RSS' can stand for either 'rich site summary' or 'really simple syndication', and both terms refer to a form of frequent updates of data by a **web feed**, such as regular news updates or notification of additions to **webpages** or **blogging** entries. Subscription to an RSS feed avoids the user requiring to manually check for any new updates.

SCREEN DUMP

Also called a screenshot, this is a copy of the image that is actually on your computer screen. It can either be printed out on paper or copied as an image and pasted into another document, such as a word-processed file. Although the image resolution of screen dumps may not be sharp, they are frequently used for instructing learners how they should progress through a sequence of tasks. A screen dump can usually be generated by depressing the 'Print Screen' key on a computer keypad and can then be pasted or

Figure 3 Example of a screen dump

printed. A screen shot has the advantage that it generates an exact image of what is on your computer screen at that instant, and so is a convenient way of guiding a new student or hesitant learner through a variety of screens or **webpages** that might seem to be quite intimidating. A common way to use screen dumps for instructing students is to direct them to a particular **URL**, then issue them with specific instructions, for example:

Go to www.uhi.ac.uk; your screen should look something like this (pages will change as they are updated).

Now click on the link to 'Academic partners' in the right-hand column and select your choice of academic partner from the list that appears in left-hand column.

Screen dumps can be used to quickly construct a guide to an **online** activity and can be disposed with or updated when the images change. They provide a simple way to ease new learners into navigating the **web** or to **download** an item from the **internet**.

SEARCH ENGINE

A search engine is a **software** application on the **internet**, the main purpose of which is to allow the user to search rapidly through the **web** in order to identify and locate documents relevant to their needs. Usually the learner will be asked to type a number of key search terms into a search box to produce a list of relevant **webpages**. The webpages will often be ranked in order of priority according to appropriate descriptive information (called **metadata**) that is used to catalogue web-based information. A straight search can be performed by typing relevant key words (such as 'rural health' for items on rural health), but the increasing popularity and extent of the web means that general searches such as this often turn up millions of supposedly relevant webpages. More specific searches can be achieved by the use of the + sign (e.g. 'rural+health+community') or by enclosing the relevant string of characters in quotation marks (e.g. 'Frank Rennie' will search only for this string of alphabetic characters). As with any key word search, choosing the most appropriate term is crucial. For example, a search for 'agriculture' will produce a different (though hopefully overlapping) set of webpages than a search for the term 'farming'.

Probably the most popular search engine currently is Google, although there are other search engines which use different algorithms to rank sites.

SELF-DIRECTED LEARNING

Also called **heutagogy**. As with many of the terms used in elearning, there is a range of concepts closely associated, if not synonymous, with self-directed learning. A list of these terms acts more or less as a definition of self-directed learning:

- **student-centred** learning;
- independent learning;
- developmental learning;
- autonomous learning;
- individualised learning;
- learner-managed learning;
- resource-based learning.

The term 'self-directed learning' came to prominence in the 1970s and 1980s, and has subsequently been somewhat devalued as simply a means of transferring the cost of learning to the learners. With the advent of elearning, however, the term, or at least the concept behind it, has become associated with the move away from teacher-directed to student-directed learning. The failure of much **computer-based training** used without any teacher support has shown the continuing importance of the teacher, but the teacher in the form of **facilitator**, rather than sage on the stage. Two of the basic premises of self-directed learning are that people need to be empowered to take personal responsibility for their own learning and that the perceived needs of learners should drive the content and design of the course.

In formal elearning, self-directed learning usually involves activities that the students carry out either individually or collaboratively. These might be problems to solve, a project to complete, a dilemma to resolve or a topic to discuss. The tutor is needed to manage the process, comment on student messages, advise and point to resource materials and generally humanise the **online** environment. In some online programmes, especially postgraduate courses, students are given more autonomy: e.g. to participate in establishing the agenda and sometimes even the **assessment**, to make choices about what they will study, to take turns moderating the discussions, to carry out peer and self-assessments, and to discover and make use of resources on the **internet**. These are all aspects of self-directed learning.

There are two elements in the establishment of a self-directed learning environment online: the willingness of the student to become self-directed, and the approach of the tutor in passing control to the students. There is evidence of resistance from both students and tutors. With students, the resistance can result from lack of skill, lack of time or lack of interest. Teacher-directed approaches are generally more familiar, easier and less time-consuming. Online collaborative activities are a prime example of self-directed learning in that students are actively involved in constructing knowledge and in creating a positive learning environment. However, they are time-consuming; they do need good team working skills and they can require students to find, analyse and present material from external resources. With online tutors, the resistance is not dissimilar: lecturing is more familiar, facilitating seems to be giving up authority and, in the initial stages, elearning can be more time-consuming than lecturing. Online tutors need to be really interested in their learners; they need to listen to them as individuals and work with them to explore viewpoints and perspectives.

Scaffolding of the process of becoming a self-directed learner is the solution most often proposed to overcome student resistance. The online course should be designed to gradually demand more and more input from the students. The tutor should set out initially to model the desired kind of commenting, questioning and reflecting that students are expected to develop. It is important that the tutor withdraws this level of commenting as the students begin to work on the activities; otherwise, they will continue to 'sit back' and wait for the tutor to comment.

Staff training and online experience are the best antidotes to tutor resistance. The skill of interacting with students online is not something for which lecturing, researching and writing academic papers are a good preparation. Tutors need to develop ways of stimulating in-depth, online **interaction**, using their understanding of the subject, their ability to identify significant ideas and question those less relevant, and their knowledge of useful resource materials. What they need to practice is the skill of encouraging students and supporting a multiplicity of perspectives, while still pushing them to examine assumptions, beliefs and ideas. Furthermore, tutors need to be able to do this through the written word and to do it with warmth, enthusiasm and respect for the individual learner.

This move to a student-centred approach is truly a two-way process. Where students have entrenched expectations about the role of the teacher, tutors can be 'compelled' by their students to adopt teacher-centred methods despite their best efforts.

It has been shown that students who have already developed self-direction in their learning – for example, those who view their success as due to their own work, those who welcome choice as an opportunity rather than a threat, and those who understand that they can learn from their peers – are most likely to be successful on elearning programmes. Not surprisingly, this type of student is more often found in postgraduates than undergraduates, in the self-confident than the unself-confident, and in mature rather than immature learners. It is not a question of age but rather of learning experience, self-perception and **motivation**. However, there is also research evidence showing that students can develop more self-direction and that elearning is an ideal vehicle for this transformation.

Informal elearning demonstrates many of the characteristics of self-directed learning. Informal learning encompasses the lifelong process of acquiring knowledge, skills, attitudes and insights from, in the case of elearning, browsing online, being a member of one or more online **communities**, buying and selling online, and using the search and **hyperlink** facilities of the **web** to investigate a subject or pursue a hobby. It is the authentic nature of this kind of learning which is most significant. Informal learners take part in these activities because they have a need or a purpose for doing it, and it is their interest and motivation that dictates the amount of time, the subject matter, the focus and their level of participation. Studies show that informal learning accounts for the great bulk of any person's lifetime learning.

SEMANTIC WEB

The Semantic Web extends the current, human-readable **web** by providing a common framework for data to be shared and reused by machines on a global scale. In short, it is a globally linked **database**. Tim Berners-Lee, inventor of the web, is the originator of the Semantic Web concept, though it is a collaborative effort led by the W3C consortia along with many other researchers and industrial partners. Their aim is to improve, extend and standardise existing systems and tools, and to develop languages for expressing information in a form which machines can process. The result should be a web which increases users' ability to find the appropriate information. Using content tags and well-defined meanings, the Semantic Web will enable computers to 'understand' what they are displaying and to communicate more effectively with each other.

The problem with the current web is that it returns tens of thousands of results, when only one is wanted. The lack of an efficient means of finding, sorting and classifying information is the problem that the Semantic Web seeks to address. When fully implemented, it promises to return fewer results but with more meaning because it is a more efficient way of relating data. The development of XML has made a fundamental contribution to its realisation through providing the foundation on which the problems of representing relationships and meaning can be built.

There is considerable controversy over the viability of the Semantic Web and the possibility of developing a machine-readable web; however, there is general agreement that if successful, it will have a radical effect on the web.

SERIOUS GAMES

A serious game is a digital or video game that has been designed to serve a particular purpose – for example, the development of specific knowledge or a specific skills set – as opposed to being a game that has been designed first and foremost for entertainment or recreation. Beyond education, serious games and **gamification** are used in sectors including health care, engineering and manufacture, defence, and for purposes including emergency planning.

SERVER

A server is a piece of computer **software** that carries out a task on behalf of another piece of software (called a **client**) such as gaining access to **email** or **webpages**. The term is now in common use to refer to the **hardware**, such as the computer, that runs the software, but this is more accurately referred to as the **web** server. In terms of popular access to the **internet**, a server functions within computer **networks** to provide a host for webpages or software applications that can be remotely accessed by users. In the context of elearning, students will connect with the school/college/university server in order to access the institutional **VLE** or **MLE**, but will most likely be aware of the existence of the server only when it ceases to function due to a technical fault (described as the server being 'down').

SIMULATION

In the context of elearning, a simulation is a learning resource that attempts to model **virtual reality** in order to illustrate a specific educational objective. Commonly, a simulation will generate a number of different scenarios in response to the user changing the initial parameters used to categorise the simulation, and may produce an **animation** to illustrate the results of this modelling. A simulation may be used to extend a **case study**, and might include **audio/video clips** and **role play** as well as web-based **graphics** and scenario-building. An advantage of a simulation in education is that it allows the manipulation of data to model outcomes in a relatively risk-free environment, or one in which learners would not normally be allowed access (e.g. potentially dangerous laboratory experiments or airline flight training).

SITUATED LEARNING

Amongst the various theories of learning, there is an argument that learning occurs best through social **interaction** as this combines a learning activity embedded within its general cultural background and the specific learning context of the knowledge. Situated learning is in contrast to classroom-based learning that tends to be based upon abstract knowledge with less reference to individual context. It is closely related to **experiential learning** and also to **activity-based learning**. Situated learning is an important facet of elearning in that it puts emphasis on the social interaction between learners as part of learning **communities** (e.g. communities of practice or communities of interest). Some theorists have proposed that situated learning is usually unintentional, rather than deliberate, as the individual learners become more involved in their community and begin to identify common values, interests and beliefs that they share.

Commonly, situated learning is focused upon problem-solving skills, or applied knowledge, and examples in the literature frequently identify situations of **peer-to-peer** learning where novices to the community share information with old-timers to their mutual advantage. The **collaborative work** and skills that are identified in studies of situated learning are similar to the key attributes in the promotion of good elearning, namely encouraging participation in the community, interactive learning activities that test the context of the learning, and clear, easily identifiable learning objectives. Learning activities are typically short and focused (c.f. a **webpage** or **learning objects**), and they may lend themselves particularly well to just-in-time learning; for example, by following relevant links via a web **browser** or portal. The link with **distributed education** is of key importance in that the learner is able to select from a variety of learning resources and learning styles in order to best suit their own individual context of learning.

SKYPE

Skype is a **software** application that makes use of the VoIP available to **broadband** users to make high-quality audio and video connections with remote contacts. In effect, Skype allows users to make 'free' telephone calls and/or connect **synchronous** video images between users. Technology such as this has a wider application for business and commercial transactions but is being incorporated in elearning **pedagogy** (see **distributed education**) due to the advantages of making learning **interaction** more immediate for remote students. It also provides a level of learner support, with the learner being able to contact the tutor or peer group for short conversations at times when help is needed.

SMARTPHONE

Many current mobile phones are actually small computers which have an inbuilt telecoms function, and they are able to perform many other tasks, such as **text messaging** or accessing **social media** to share data. Commonly, they run using **software** called **apps** ('applications'), which perform specific functions such as giving access to **Facebook**, or other **network** tasks, including **mobile learning** and **surfing** the **internet**.

SNAIL MAIL

A derogatory term for the conventional post delivery services of letters and other communications and used to emphasise the slow speed of delivery of paper-based communications in comparison to the almost-instantaneous delivery of **email** or **text messaging**. Despite this, postal delivery of course materials and other resources continues to be used as a complement to electronic versions and/or as a backup (e.g. a tutor may post a CD with course materials as well as making this available on an **MLE** or another **webpage**). The advantages of this are that learners are not entirely dependent upon accessing their learning resources solely via the **internet**, and that they can combine the convenience of both electronic and hard copies.

SOCIAL BOOKMARKING

This is a form of **tagging** which allows users of **networks** which are **online** to identify useful resources on the **web**, then share, sort and store the bookmarks to allow easy return access. Some social bookmarking services allow users to link to a **web feed** to enable regular updating of information, and to group tags into a **folksonomy** in order to sort or classify the resources and share with fellow users of the service.

SOCIAL CAPITAL

This is a hotly debated social science term that is used to describe the collective value of networks of **trust**, mutual understanding and reciprocal help that facilitate coordination and cooperation in **communities** for mutual benefit. In the 1990s, some social scientists began to look at the nature of community in a different way. They made the case that the more strongly people identify themselves by their membership of a community, and the more they feel that they have a full role to play in the life and decision-making roles of their community, then the more strongly that group actually functions as a community. It has been suggested that if economic capital resides in people's bank accounts, and human capital is inside their heads, then social capital is vested in the structure of their relationships. People's sense of community is derived from their perception of being linked into a complex system of relationships and **interaction**, and these shared experiences help to foster group solidarity and a sense of common purpose. This is a key advantage in **online** learning communities, where participants rarely know each other, may never meet, and may have little in common apart from their interest in the subject being studied.

By acting together in a common space, members of a community learn from each other to foster a sense of collective identity, which they seek to define and reinforce by constructing 'rules' of behaviour (however rigid or loose) through which they can achieve a general consensus that is consistent with their common interests. The ways by which these norms are constructed, reinforced and enforced will be different between different communities, and this is as true between geographical communities as it is between geographical and 'virtual' communities. Networking is a vital component of community development, and in this respect online communities offer advantages over geographical 'communities of place' because distributed community members are able to overcome the necessity of being in the same location and/or active at the same time to engage in collective dialogue or decision-making.

A key community-building element resulting from social networking is the fostering of trust between the members of the **network**, partly from sharing stories and partly through being exposed to the stories of participants who seem to be similar to themselves in some ways but different in other ways. The **web** has emerged as a new technological vehicle for harvesting the personal experiences of others, and the construction of tools that attempt to make this collective activity more visible (and accessible) is a major research field. Studies show that reciprocal support is a vital part of community networks, both online and in a physical location, though this may manifest itself in a wide range of ways, from baby-sitting, to practical comfort in times of stress, to the praise and celebration of a successful task well done. At the heart of collaborative activity, there is an understanding that participants contribute something positive when they are able to, in the realisation that they may be required to draw on the support of others at some point in the future. Social capital, sometimes referred to as 'the glue that holds a community together', increases a community's productive potential in several ways, by sharing ideas, resources and expertise, by networking information more quickly, and by encouraging **peer-to-peer** learning as well as collective responsibility. This is an important aspect of **collaborative learning** activities, and the many-to-many **accessibility** of online interactive networks means that 'virtual communities' have profound implications, not simply for learning but for understanding social change in general.

SOCIAL MEDIA

Any form of technology, usually digital, which enables accessing, creating and sharing of information, including text, images, video, and so on.

Typically, social media uses the **web** to enable communications using devices such as a **smartphone**, or a **tablet**, or a **laptop.** The use of social media for such purposes is also called **social networking**, although the actual communications may be one-to-one, as well as one-to-many and many-to-many. Common social media services include **Twitter** and **Facebook**, but there are many hundreds of services based on a digital **app**.

SOCIAL NETWORKING

Social networking involves the use of digital devices and **web-based** services to connect to a **network** of widely dispersed individuals or groups in order to share and co-create information. It is widely used for personal and recreational purposes, and in some business activities such as product promotion, but due to **data security** concerns, its use is in its infancy for **mobile learning** and **flexible learning**.

SOCIAL PRESENCE

In relation to digital education, social presence relates to various dimensions in which individuals can feel a sense of (or be perceived as) 'being there' in terms of their virtual presence. This can encompass: the illusion of being there – for example, through being connected or co-located within or through a digital space or environment; the feeling of being there as an active participant in an **asynchronous** or synchronous digital space or environment, including interacting and working with others; and social presence in relation feeling an affinity with, and sharing a 'sense of belonging' with, others in the environment.

Fostering and experience a sense of social presence is well established as a key factor in supporting engagement, **retention** and achievement in **online** learning programmes.

The above is adapted and extended from the definition of 'social presence' offered by edutechwiki (http://edutechwiki.unige.ch/en/Social_presence)

SOFTWARE

Any computer programme or set of organised instructions designed to make an electronic device (such as a computer or a printer) perform in a deliberate manner. The software is normally hosted on some physical infrastructure termed the **hardware**, and is purchased separately from the hardware (although retailers are now commonly selling a 'bundle' of hardware plus basic software to new users). Typical software applications include the common computer programmes that are used to do word-processing, **database** compilation, or to connect to the **internet** to send **email** or do some **surfing**.

SPAM

Although this term was originally used as a slang expression for the practice of sending an excessive amount of data to a computer system in order to make it crash (cease to function), it has come to mean any unwanted and unsolicited **post** to a **discussion board** or **email** in-tray. Common spam includes advertisements for various unwanted products or attempts to get recipients to sign up for events and activities that they would normally avoid. Apart from the nuisance value of spam – since every message has to be read, or at least identified, before it can be deleted – the objections to spam are that it slows down network performance by taking up memory space and **bandwidth** with unnecessary (and unwanted) messages. Most **ISPs** now include a routine spam filter as part of their service to customers, although of course spammers are constantly inventing new ways to break through the barriers.

STACK EXCHANGE

Stack Exchange was established in 2010 as an online Q&A community for computer programmers and developers. There are now over 170 Q&A communities on Stack Exchange, covering a vast range of topics and areas of practice and expertise in technology, culture and recreation, life and arts, science and business.

Each Stack Exchange Q&A community is built by experts and allows members to ask questions of that community. In turn, the members of that community can vote on posts offered in response to questions, which ranks the quality and usefulness of the answers so the most valuable answers are the most visible. Using many of the principles of **gamification** in the design of the Stack Exchange **platform**, those providing answers can 'unlock' certain privileges and earn **digital badges** for posting answers that others have found useful.

Stack Exchange is a prominent example of how **social networking** technologies and aspects of gamification can be harnessed to facilitate the crowdsourcing of knowledge from within professional and disciplinary **networks** that sit beyond formal educational institutions.

STALKING

The practice of an individual monitoring, observing and/or communicating with another individual **online** in a manner which is unsought and unwanted. A stalker may or may not also be a **troll**, and in some countries stalking on the **internet** is a criminal offence. Institutions normally protect people engaged in **online learning** by the administration of a **firewall** and by the application of **netiquette** regulations, but any such abuse should be reported.

STUDENT-CENTRED LEARNING/ LEARNER-CENTRED LEARNING

This is an approach to teaching in which the experience of the learner is central. The focus is on how the students are learning, what they experience and how they engage in the learning process. Through a process of gradual empowerment, student-centred learning focuses on student outcomes rather than on teaching. While references to student-centred learning abound in the literature, definitions are often confused with other teaching strategies. A range of similar terms are:

Teacher-centred learning	Student-centred learning
Teacher prescribes learning goals and objectives based on prior experiences, past practices and existing mandated standards.	Students work with teachers to select learning goals and objectives based on authentic problems and students' prior knowledge, interests and experience.
Students expect teachers to teach them what's required to pass the test. Passive recipients of information. Reconstructs knowledge and information.	Teacher provides multiple means of accessing information and acts as facilitator, helps students access and process information.
Teacher organises and presents information to groups of students and acts as gatekeeper of knowledge, controlling student's access to information.	Students take responsibility for learning. Active knowledge seekers. Construct knowledge and meaning.
Assessment used to sort students. Exams used to assess stuents' acquisition of information. Teacher sets performance criteria for students.	Assessment is an integral part of learning. Performance-based, used to assess students' ability to apply knowledge. Students develop self-assessment and peer assessment skills.
Teachers serve as the centre of epistemological knowledge, directing the learning process and controlling student's access to information. Students viewed as 'empty' vessels and learning is viewed as an additive process. Instruction is geared for the 'average' student and everyone is forced to progress at the same rate.	Learning is an active dynamic process in which connections are constantly changing and their structure is continually reformatted. Students construct their own meaning by talking, listening, writing, reading, and reflecting on content, ideas, issues and concerns.

Figure 4 Contrast between teacher–centred and student–centred learning

- **self-directed learning**;
- learner-focused learning;
- autonomous learning;
- independent learning;

- **collaborative learning**;
- **experiential learning**;
- authentic learning;
- **problem-based learning**;
- constructivist learning.

To generalise about all of these terms, it is possible to say that they give students greater autonomy and control over choice of subject matter, learning methods or pace of study. Some student-centred approaches concentrate on giving students more input into:

- what is learned;
- how it is learned; or
- when it is learned.

An important implication of this definition is that students need to assume a high level of responsibility in the learning situation and be actively choosing their goals and managing their learning. They can no longer rely on the lecturer to tell them what, how, where and when to think. Many students – in particular, surface learners – tend to want to be told what to do and what to think. There is often a feeling amongst students that the tutor has been paid to teach and should set about teaching. The tradition of 'telling as teaching' is strong. How far is one prepared to move from this tradition towards more student-centred approaches and risk poor appraisals by students?

Student-centred learning is often contrasted with teacher-centred learning, as Figure 4 summarises.

SURFING

The procedure of navigating over the **web** using a **search engine** to display and select **webpages** that are of interest to the user. Surfing is sometimes also called 'browsing' due to the fact that **software** called a web **browser** is used to connect the user's computer with the search engine and then display the results.

SYNCHRONOUS LEARNING

Learning activities are synchronous when they allow learners to have a level of **interactivity** at the same moment of time, e.g. a **face-to-face (f2f)** meeting, a live **videoconference**, a telephone conversation or an **audioconference** discussion. Due to the fact that elearning and **distributed education** in general allow for a wide diversity of **asynchronous learning** activities, it is usual to qualify whether a 'meeting' of learners (and tutors) is planned to occur synchronously or asynchronously. It is common to refer to a mix of synchronous and asynchronous learning activities (e.g. **online learning** plus face-to-face lectures) as **blended learning**, although there is a blurring of the boundaries with distributed education.

TABLET

A tablet is a form of portable computer, usually with a thin, flat screen, mid-way in size between a **laptop** computer and a **smartphone**. A typical example is an iPad. Tablets are commonly used for **mobile learning**.

TAGGING

Tagging is the process of adding labels, or 'tags', to digital artefacts (including blog posts, social media posts, photos and video) in order to categorise them to make it easier to search for and/or share them. The attachment of tags to **posts** on **social media**, such as **blogs** or **social bookmarking** sites, can be a convenient method of sorting and finding useful data that you have previously accessed. Tagging is a common feature in websites meant to encourage sharing, such as in **Creative Commons**, and on sites which aggregate **open educational resources**. Tags can be user defined (for example, an author creating and adding tags that correspond to key terms in a blog post they are about to publish) or can be selected from pre-defined tags (for example, using the options to tag friends and locations in a status update to be posted to **Facebook**). Tags can also be added into the content of web pages when they are being created.

Tags serve multiple functions. They allow **search engines** to locate and index the content of websites and blog **posts**, and they allow readers to select and view all the content (for example, from a blog they are reading) that corresponds to specific tags. Tags also alert fellow users to the fact that they have been featured (or tagged) in a **social media** post. In **Twitter**, the tagging of topics or events in a Twitter post is managed through the use of **hashtags**, while fellow users are tagged through the inclusion of their Twitter 'handle' (e.g. @frankrennie) in a post.

TEXT MESSAGING

Although this term can be applied to any textual form of communication, such as **email**, it is generally now only applied to short message service (SMS) messages via mobile phones. Also called 'texting' or 'txt', there are currently relatively few text messaging applications specifically for elearning due largely to the reliance on a small hand-held screen. Text messaging has enjoyed a phenomenal growth over the past few years, especially amongst young people, and some student services facilities have sought to capitalise upon this, e.g. by sending library notifications or overdue notices by text messaging to students' mobile phones.

THREADED DISCUSSION

A threaded discussion is a series of messages on a particular topic **posted** in a **discussion board** forum. These discussions are **asynchronous** and the conversations occur amongst a group of learners. 'Threads' allow the reader to follow the various contributions to the discussion and respond to specific messages. A running log is thus created of remarks and opinions which build up over time. Users **email** their comments, and the computer maintains them in order of originating message and then replies to that message. The educational applications are:

- Good for supporting thoughtful responses where reflection is warranted;
- Appropriate where **face-to-face** (**f2f**) opportunities are limited or impossible;
- Easy to integrate with other **online** or offline activities;
- Can be particularly useful with quiet or reflective learners who might not participate in a classroom discussion.

Successful educational discussions usually require careful guidance and structure from the instructor. Examples of useful approaches include: providing timelines for the discussion, some form of accountability, and specific tasks or roles for each participant. Debates are one useful structure; student presentations are another. Although the teacher provides the overall guidance, it is important that students feel they control the **interaction** and have the opportunity to develop their own understanding of the issues. Offering students the chance to moderate the discussion for a period can be a good way of giving students just this opportunity.

Part of the educational benefit of this kind of discussion is the exposure students get to different perspectives and varying interpretations by reading the various threads. There is research evidence that the asynchronous nature of threaded discussion offers valuable time for reflection, which can in turn lead to higher order thinking: exploring, integrating and resolving issues. There is disagreement about whether it is advisable to award students marks for the nature or number of postings. On the one hand, it encourages participation; on the other, it can lead to students writing for the teacher.

Threaded discussions are used in **chatrooms** on the **internet** and on **online** services as well as in groupware products.

TUTOR MARKED ASSIGNMENT (TMA)

A tutor marked assignment is a piece of work submitted to a course tutor by a learner for marking as part of a structured learning experience. Normally the learner will get some **feedback** from the tutor, as well as a mark or grade that can be used to assess their performance and/or understanding of the course. A TMA can range very widely in style to cover essays, reports, book reviews, individual or group projects, presentations and a variety of other forms of measuring learners' levels of understanding. Diversity in the type of TMA can support the different needs of learners and links positively with the diversity of resources available in **distributed education**. TMA contrasts with CMA (computer marked assignment).

TOOLBAR

This is usually a row or column of **icons** that are displayed at the top, bottom or side of a computer screen to allow quick and easy navigation to other **software** (such as another office application), tasks (such as printing or saving) or other locations (such as a folder or an additional drive). The toolbar can usually be customised to appear on the **desktop** when the user decides to **logon**, and often the choice of icons or task buttons can be selected by the user to display a palette of the user's most common tasks or software applications. Individual software applications may have their own toolbars to allow easy navigation when using them.

TROJAN

This is a type of computer **virus** that is designed to be deliberately destructive to computer files and/or their operating systems. It was initially named after the 'Trojan horse' of Greek mythology due to the fact that the virus was concealed within other files that masqueraded as games or pieces of useful information. Unlike a **worm**, the Trojan is specifically created to cause damage to the users of computer **networks**, but a good, modern, virus protection **software** hosted by most reputable **ISPs** should be sufficient safeguard for most users.

TROLL

An informal term for a person who uses the **internet** to start arguments or other quarrelsome distractions on **online** services and/

or **social media** spaces. In **online learning**, trolls may initially be controlled by referring to an agreed **netiquette**, but if the abuse continues, it may become necessary to suspend the troll from the service.

TRUST

A key element in the construction of online **communities** resulting from social networking is the fostering of trust between the members of the **network**. Learning activities that encourage learner interaction, through **discussion boards** or collaborative activities, can also stimulate the development of trust, and this is important in several ways. In the first instance, learners are encouraged to participate more fully when they have a measure of trust in their fellow participants (e.g. that their contributions to the discussion will be valued and not be ridiculed). Second, trust is important for the establishment of **peer-to-peer** learning whereby learners can share experiences and come to regard each other as trusted sources of knowledge. Two components are key to the formation of this trust: reliability and reciprocity. Obviously, it is important that shared information is reliable and can contribute towards the learning experience, and in this context trust can be accumulated in a participant who consistently supplies accurate information, or lost by the supply of less reliable contributions. It is interesting to note that some **online** auction facilities, such as eBay, award a rating to participants based upon **feedback** on the quality of their services, reliability, promptness, and so on. In terms of reciprocity, if the participants in group-learning activities feel in some way that their help to others might be returned at some point in the future, this can act as a powerful bonding force in the group.

Trust also has wider connotations; for example, that information divulged online will not be misused, or that apparently valuable sources of information such as a useful **website**, a specialist portal giving access to themed information sources, or reports provided by individual **blogging** enthusiasts are in fact what they claim to be. The **web** has emerged as a new technological vehicle for harvesting the personal experiences of others, and the construction of tools that attempt to make this collective activity more visible (and accessible) is a major research field.

TUTOR GROUP

This is a group of students assigned to a particular tutor who guides them through an **internet** learning experience. The primary role of the tutor is to develop a rapport with the students and add a human touch to the process of learning. Responsibilities of the tutor vary but usually involve encouraging discussions, exploring ideas and commenting on students' messages. Students in the group may work collaboratively and may be asked to take leadership roles, such as leading a discussion, in order to develop **online** skills. **Interaction** can be through **discussion boards, chatrooms, email, audioconferencing** or text and **webpages**. Communication can be one-to-one with the tutor or another student, or one-to-many with the whole tutor group.

Many students form close attachments with the other students in the tutor group through sharing problems, solutions and resources. **Online** tutors need to prioritise their workload, as students can be overly demanding. Their key aim is to build student confidence and develop their understanding of the material.

The success of the tutor group as a learning environment is partially dependent on the input of the tutor and partially on the design of the course. The attitude of the tutor is evident in the extent to which:

- they value and encourage students' ideas and questions;
- they see students as partners in a learning journey;
- they share their field of expertise;
- they actively search for ways to help students learn.

The design of the course also has an impact on the working of the tutor group:

- Learning activities – opportunities are generated for students to explore their own hypotheses, promoting scholarly and reflective practices consistent with skill development as **lifelong learners**;
- **Assessment** – methods are designed to be fair and give opportunities for different kinds of learners to show what they know;
- Support materials – formal communications (subject guides, learning outcomes and assessment guidelines, timetables, etc.) are clear, specific and in writing.

TUTORING

Tutoring **online** – or e-moderating, as it is sometimes called – involves the support, management and **assessment** of students in an elearning environment. It is generally accepted that the effort and skill of the tutor are the key to successful **online** learning. In some cases, the tutor is also the instructor who develops the course or programme, usually from a **face-to-face** (**f2f**) mode to the online mode, or to a **blended** mode. In other cases, the content and **web** development are carried out by a team of people, each expert in different aspects of the process (e.g. web design, **pedagogy** and administration).

Tutoring online primarily requires a change of attitude from lecturing face-to-face, in that the tutor is not in control of the situation to the same extent as the lecturer in front of a class. The tutor's role is much closer to that of a **facilitator**, supporting students, guiding them to resources, advising about assignments and managing the online environment. The latter might involve setting up new discussion areas as required, keeping track of student progress and assessment results, or initiating collaborative activities. In some contexts, the tutor may be expected to use **videoconferencing** or **audioconferencing**, or communicate one-to-one with students by telephone. The main task of the tutor, however, is to be the subject expert, summarising discussion topics, correcting misunderstandings and marking assignments. Social skills are more important online than they are in face-to-face teaching. Tutors need to be engaging, reassuring, welcoming and supporting. They also need to make sure that the online discussion areas are not dominated by one or two students, and that shy and unconfident students are encouraged to participate.

There are many courses offered online in how to tutor. However, the most valuable learning is through practice and experience of the online environment. Taking an online course and experiencing the process of being an online student can be a good way of developing a sensitivity for online learning. Just as students need to become comfortable interacting online, perhaps with people they never meet, so the tutor needs to establish an individual tutoring style that feels comfortable. Many teaching skills are as applicable online as face-to-face, including the ability to explain topics clearly and to provide useful **feedback** to students on their assignments, and enthusiasm for the subject area. Additional skills needed to teach online are: willingness to engage with students in their learning process, ability to facilitate group discussions and flexibility in responding to the unpredictability of the medium. The online environment has strengths and weaknesses, and the tutor needs to be aware of these and find ways of maximising the benefits and minimising the limitations of the medium.

Online tutors, like elearners, need to develop their understanding of what the **web** can offer and their ability to find and assess the value of web resources. The web may be the richest, most varied and easily accessed information source that has ever been available, but developing the skill to discriminate between a good website and a poor one is something that tutors and elearners both need to address. Amongst other things, they need to consider the accuracy and depth of information, visual attractiveness and relevance to the course.

There are a number of crucial tasks for the tutor to perform at the beginning of an online course:

1. It is important for tutors to make clear what their students can expect from them (e.g. how often and when they will **log on**, what level of support they will provide and where to put their technical queries).

2. An **email** message from the tutor to each student at the beginning or even before the start of the course is highly recommended. This might contain an introduction to the course, any essential administrative information and some background about the tutor, but most important is the reassuring tone established by the message. Although most of the content will be the same for each learner, it is ideal if the tutor sends this initial message to each student individually, addressing them by name and perhaps noting any details about the student gained from the registration information.

3. Tutors should devote more time to online **interaction** in the initial phase of the course than at any subsequent phase. For example, as each student enters the **discussion board** area, tutors should make sure that a response is made either by another student or by making one themselves. Students feel particularly vulnerable about communicating 'in public' at the beginning of a course and need encouragement and reassurance that they are on the right track. Likewise, it is important at the beginning of the course that tutors answer any email promptly. If the learner poses a question that cannot be answered quickly then the tutor should send a holding reply, acknowledging receipt of the email and explaining that they will answer as soon as possible, ideally giving some indication of when that will be.

4. Messages arising from the early activities also need more comments from the tutor until the process of peer commenting is established. In the first phase of the course, the tutor is modelling this skill of giving feedback. Comments should be positive yet honest and challenging. This is part of the process of developing **trust**, which is an essential component of online **community**.

The skill of the online tutor is in developing a way of responding to online discussions that is constructive and encouraging, but also that challenges the learners by asking relevant questions that will move the group forward in their learning. This questioning approach must be conducted with tact and care. It must neither seem like an interrogation nor like a list of set questions that are not tailored to the group. Too many questions can be overwhelming and students rarely answer any of them. One or two questions per message are enough. It is often useful if the tutor provides some indication of how a question could be answered or gives a personal view or opinion. This allows the learners a hook on which to hang their response.

TWEET

A short **post** in the **social media** site, **Twitter**.

TWITTER

Twitter is a free-to-use **micro-blogging, social networking** service that allows registered users to submit short text-based posts (called **Tweets**) of up to 280 characters (although this was originally limited to 140). Tweets can include images or links to videos, and the user can opt to use **hashtags** to refer to particular topics or events so that their Tweets are discoverable by other users who are interested in or are sharing their own views using the same hashtag.

The term 'Tweet-up' is often used to refer to a real-time Twitter gathering in which users interested in the same subjects come together for a facilitated Twitter Q&A session. Tweet-ups are used widely by various groups in the education sector; for example, those facilitated by @LTHEchat (Learning and Teaching in Higher Education) using the #lthechat hashtag.

Other uses of Twitter in education include following relevant organisations, learned societies, research groups and expert scholars, to allow educators and learners to keep up with thinking and research in their discipline area, and for networking amongst PhD students.

UPLOAD

Uploading involves the transfer of data from one computer onto another computer or **network**. This term is often confused with the term '**download**'. A common occurrence for elearners is the need to upload their **TMA** or other pieces of pre-prepared text onto a **discussion board** or some other section of an **MLE**. Normally this is achieved simply by sending an **email** to the relevant site and adding the TMA as an **attachment**. The ability to upload data is similar to the constraints on downloading (i.e. small, simple files are transferred quickly and easily, but larger, more complex files often require **broadband** to function efficiently). Usually the **internet** connection is **asynchronous** in its **bandwidth**, with the property of being able to download data at a faster rate than it is possible to upload the same data. This is due to the fact that the network is designed to **surf** the **web** and receive data, rather than send out large volumes of data from a domestic computer.

URL

Commonly also called 'web addresses', the uniform resource locator (URL) is a standardised address for **web** resources that both identifies the resource and tells how to find it. In many ways, a URL is the basic building block of the web as far as individual users are concerned as it specifies the specific location of each individual resource on the web in a generic format that is unique to that particular resource but can also be extended to include other similar resources. An example of this might indicate an article stored as a document or a **PDF** file, in a certain folder, on a particular **server**, hosted by a named organisation, in a certain country. The URL for my **homepage** within my institution is at the following address: www.lews.uhi.ac.uk/frennie.

VALIDATION

This is a general term that refers to the **quality assurance** process for approving a degree or similar academic award. The validation process will normally consist of a thorough testing of all aspects of the award, including **course design**, appropriate resources, methods of delivery and **assessment**, staff expertise and the contents/context of the learning materials. This would include access to any **online libraries** and **MLE** that would be available to the prospective learners. The scrutiny may or may not be conducted by specialists who are external to the awarding-giving body, in collaboration with the normal quality assurance process of the institution. Normally the validation process for online components of an award will be incorporated with, and seamless with, the approval of 'non-online' components, but an unfamiliarity with the theory and practice of **elearning** may sometimes result in the validation panel applying a more rigid quality assurance standard than would be expected for **face-to-face** (**f2f**) delivery.

VIDEOCONFERENCING

As elearning has shifted its interpretation into electronic media other than simply **email** interacting with a set of **web** resources, it has come to include videoconferencing as part of the array of **online** resources. At its simplest, this has been described as a method of conferencing between two or more locations where both sound and vision are conveyed electronically so as to enable simultaneous interactive communication. It is possible to use the **internet** to connect videoconference sites, but due to technical restrictions on data transfer many institutions prefer to use an Integrated Services Digital Network (ISDN) that provides high-quality data transmission in real time through normal dial-up connections (i.e. without the need for expensive dedicated lines). It is not a new technology, but improvements in equipment, dramatic lowering of the operational costs and the increasing availability of dial-up connections have produced a rapid growth in its use. Multinational companies have been using elements of videoconferencing since the 1960s, but it is really only since the mid-1990s that there has been other than experimental use by educational establishments. Essentially, there are four main uses of videoconferencing in education:

1. Meetings. Bringing together peers that are distributed over a wide geographical area for whom **face-to-face** (**f2f**) meetings would be costly or prohibitive. This would include supervision meetings with research students located on a campus remote from their supervisor, and also video counselling for remote students. There has been an upsurge of videoconferencing for meetings in the aftermath of the September 11th attacks as it is perceived to allow the benefits of visual communication without the necessity of air travel.

2. Teaching. The etiquette of small-group teaching has much in common with the requirements of videoconferencing and has proved a very popular medium for reaching students who are scattered on distributed sites. Initial use simply to replicate a face-to-face lecture has been recognised as counterproductive and this has resulted in a more strategic approach to the use of videoconferencing for teaching. The network communications enable a specialist tutor to contribute from a location other than that of the students (another college, a hospital or laboratory) and this has proved popular with multi-campus universities. It is useful for occasional short presentations by an international specialist to add variety and/or costly detail to a course. It has the additional advantage over **audioconferencing** that it can display a range of visual resources such as PowerPoint slides and documents via overhead camera, as well as the emotional reactions of students.

3. Management. Course committees and other educational bureaucracy can be effectively conducted via videoconference, especially where multi-campus institutions would otherwise incur significant travel costs. The conduct of videoconference meetings requires some additional social considerations to be most effective (see **netiquette**).

4.   Interviews. Using **videoconferencing** for interviewing has extended the reach beyond simply face-to-face interviews, particularly when considering international applicants for research positions or faculty posts where cost is a consideration.

The main advantages of videoconferencing lie in the ability to link one-to-one or multi-point connections for short, intense contacts that would otherwise be prohibitively expensive to facilitate. It can also be a rich source of learning content, particularly when combined with other learning resources. Disadvantages are that the costs of high-quality equipment still restrict its use to key locations, and that poorer-quality connections may result in jerky movements and a time-lag in audio transmission, creating a learning environment that is less spontaneous than face-to-face meetings. Experience shows that videoconference sessions work better between people who have met before, even briefly, and for focused tasks. As a result, the use of videoconference sessions seems to work best intermittently and in combination with other **blended learning** resources for participants who are geographically distributed. This entails bringing participants together synchronously for strategically focused learning events rather than as a standard replacement for lecture presentations.

VIRTUAL REALITY

An effect using computer **software** to create a **simulation** of reality, initially created as an environment of total immersion, and speedily adopted for use in **serious games** and **gamification**. Best-known examples would include various types of flight simulator programmes that give the feeling of actually flying an aircraft, or programmes for constructing buildings in 3D that allow users to navigate through the rooms and are used by the emergency services and military for practicing rescue techniques. With the wider availability of **broadband**, there is increasing interest in elearning to exploit virtual reality techniques and **augmented reality** to create educational simulations such as 'virtual field trips' that allow learners to 'visit' sites such as landscapes, geological sites, laboratories, or nuclear reactors that would be difficult or impossible for the student to visit in real life.

VIRTUAL SEMINAR

Sometimes also called a **webinar**, this is an **online** form of academic seminar that is extended over a specified period of time, perhaps one to three days, to provide an **asynchronous learning** experience over the **web**. Normally a virtual seminar is dedicated to a specific topic of study and is conducted through a **discussion board** on a **VLE** with a small group of more advanced learners. Commonly a presentation is given, or there is a piece of set reading to which learners are asked to respond and actively challenge. Key elements of a virtual seminar are that the learning experience encourages **interaction**, that **peer-to-peer** learning is supported, and that the activity is **online**, facilitated by **ICT**. In contrast to a **webcast**, which is one-directional, a webinar promotes and supports multiple connections, including in some cases **email** messages and **audioconference** links with the virtual seminar site, which may later be translated into **text messages** on the discussion board. Some use the term 'virtual seminar' to include seminars conducted by **videoconference**, but though the boundaries may be blurred, the term 'webinar' explicitly requires the use of web-based **software** applications for participation.

VIRTUAL UNIVERSITY

This concept rose to prominence in the 1990s as a means of offering students maximum flexibility, independence and, in some instances, individual services. The term denotes a university that uses predominantly virtual learning processes as well as examination and administrative services. In some cases, the virtual university is a consortium of participating institutions. A range of **synchronous** and **asynchronous** communication technologies are an integral feature of most such universities. Communication amongst the students and faculty is a central feature of the learning process, though in some instances the teaching method is self-study of course materials. **Online library** resources and teaching material which could consist of **animations, simulations, video clips** or **learning objects** are the other main components of the virtual offering. Some virtual teaching is by video lectures, accessed by the students either synchronously or asynchronously.

Peer learning and collaborative activities, **online** seminars and pre-sentations, guest lectures and **webcasts** are the main teaching methods.

Online registration for new and returning students is usually supported, as is course choice and access to personal information, academic results and financial status. Some virtual universities have also implemented online payment, so that the student never has to come to the university. The wave of enthusiasm for virtual universities has now largely dissipated, and although there are still institutions using the word 'virtual' in their title, and even new institutions being proposed, research evidence combined with practical experience favours **blended** approaches. Furthermore, the once-separate models of distance and on-campus teaching are converging with the applications of **ICT** so that educational functions such as programme and course development, delivery to students, provision of learner support and administration are at most universities a blend of virtual and place-based procedures. Virtual universities have found a niche in the education system: for specialist areas, for postgraduates and work-related degrees, for very small countries or small universities to band together to seek econo-mies of scale.

VIRUS

A computer programme that has the ability to replicate itself, spread through computer **networks** (usually attached to **email**) and affect the host computer in a particular manner. The rising popularity of the **internet** produces ideal conditions for a virus to multiply and spread from computer to computer, and though some, such as a **Trojan**, are created to cause deliberate damage, many viruses, such as a **worm**, are written to generate **spam** and/or cause a nuisance to individual com-puter users. Many viruses are created simply to spread panic and anxiety about security issues amongst less-informed computer users, and many virus 'scares' are simply hoaxes.

Increasingly sophisticated anti-virus **software** provided by **ISP** com-panies can scan and block many suspect communications, but of course the perpetrators creating viruses have responded by seeking new ways to circumvent anti-virus software. Although viruses are usually quite mild in their effect, and are not intrinsically damaging in themselves, the cumulative damage that they can cause through overstressing **servers**, filling memory space and time-wasting at work means that the transmission of viruses result in millions of pounds worth of losses to businesses worldwide. Most educational institutes combine a system **firewall** with anti-virus scanning software and **password** protection to their **VLE** or **MLE** in order to provide maximum security and comfort for elearners.

VLE

This is an abbreviation for 'virtual learning environment', meaning the mix of **hardware** and **software** that is used to create **online** learning opportunities outside of the classroom situation. The term originated in a similar context to **virtual reality** constructions, in which education- alists attempted to create a learning environment where learners engaged with learning resources and tutors in a manner that was markedly different to the conventional classroom or lecture hall, yet which seemed to contain familiar educational components. In this manner:

- Conventional lecture notes might become **webpages** of short, structured guides to educational topics, with **hyperlinks** to take learners to additional resources;
- Course handouts might be **digitized** and added to the VLE as backup documents for further reading;
- Tests and formative **assessments** can be shared amongst all learners, regardless of their geographical locality;
- A **discussion board** might be used to promote **interactive** dialo- gue between students and staff in a similar manner to an extended classroom conversation;
- Learners have the ability to exchange information in small **tutorial groups** and/or individually by **email** or by **instant messaging** facilities that help to reduce the feeling of working alone.

In short, the VLE attempts to emulate all aspects of the students' learning environment, but in an online manner using **ICT** and, normally, a computer **network** such as the **internet** or a college/ university **intranet**. A number of commercial VLEs are available for purchase (e.g. Blackboard, Canvas, D2L) as well as a growing number of **open source** solutions. Although the term 'VLE' is still frequently used for convenience, as the VLEs become more sophisticated and 'user friendly' there has been a tendency to resist the term '*virtual* learning environment' on the grounds that a *real* learning environment has been created, though it differs markedly from what has been considered as conventional education, i.e. **face-to-face** (**f2f**) education in a classroom or lecture theatre. This has led to the more popular use of the term 'managed learning environment' (**MLE**) that combines all of the elements of a good VLE with the addition of organisational management **software** tools such as access to the university's student information system, email, secure intranet, **online library** facilities and other educational management facilities that are not directly related to the activities of teaching and learning.

VODCAST

This is a form of **social media** communication, (also called vlogging) similar to a **podcast**, by which short **video clips** are shared. As with podcasts, a mobile device such as a **smartphone** or a **tablet** is the most common form of access to vodcasts.

WEB

A shortened version of the term 'World Wide Web', that refers to the enormous, interlinked collection of files, or 'documents', that are made available to people over the **internet**. These **webpages** are easy to create with appropriate **software** and can contain a huge range of information in the form of text, **graphics** and video or audio files. Webpages are connected via **hyperlinks** that enable users to 'jump' from one page to another, following the users' interests – an activity known as **surfing**. The contents of the web can be scrutinised by using a **search engine** to look for key words in the users' area of interest, producing a list of sites from which the most appropriate webpages can be selected to view. The 'address' of a page on the web is referred to as its **URL**.

WEB 2.0

A shorthand term that refers to the second-generation development of the **Web**, which saw a move away from static **webpages** to dynamically and user generated content, the emergence of read-write web applications including **blogs** and **Wikis**, and the advent of **social networking**.

WEB-BASED LEARNING

'Web-based learning' is another synonym for 'elearning' or '**online** learning'. Course content is easily delivered on the **web**, and discussion forums via **email, videoconferencing, discussion boards** and live lectures (videostreaming) are all possible. One of the values of using the web to access course materials is that **webpages** may contain **hyperlinks** to other parts of the web, thus enabling access to a vast amount of web-based information.

Most web-based courses use a virtual learning environment (**VLE**) or managed learning environment (**MLE**), as these combine the functions of discussions, real-time **chatrooms**, online **assessment**, tracking of students' use of the web and course administration, as well as course content. Several approaches can be used to develop and deliver web-based learning. At one end is 'pure' distance learning (in which course material, assessment and support is all delivered online, with no **face-to-face** contact between students and teachers). At the other end is an organisational **intranet**, which replicates printed course materials online to support what is essentially a traditional face-to-face course. The latter is usually referred to as **blended learning**.

Features of a typical web-based course are:

- teaching material including links to related information and articles, e.g. online **databases**, journals, library;
- course information, timetable, course guide;
- formative and summative assessments;
- student management tools (records, statistics, student tracking);
- discussion areas, email and real-time chat facilities.

WEB ENABLED

This is a technical term indicating that an object (or, in some cases, an organisation) is able to interact with the World Wide **Web** over the **internet**, frequently, but not always, over a **wireless network**. Celebrated examples of web enabled artefacts include statues, paintings and museum exhibits that also have a **web presence** that gives more detailed information, interpretation, etc., on the work of art. Some examples of smart textiles and smart clothing have been developed in pursuit of **virtual reality** that allows the user to interact with their environment and/or to simulate real-life conditions in unusual situations, such as giving the illusion of close proximity between collaborators remote from each other. Web enabled objects have been proposed as useful learning resources that will extend the notion of ubiquitous learning and opportunities for **mobile learning** (i.e. structured learning opportunities while using a **laptop** computer/personal digital assistant/mobile phone while the user is on the move).

WEB FEED

An automated computer system for supplying regular updates of information from the web, straight to a user. The topics of information, such as newsflashes or sports stories, are selected by the user in advance and then pulled to the **smartphone** or other device as the information becomes available. Web feeds have a similar function to **RSS** feeds but not every web feed uses RSS protocols.

WEB PRESENCE

This is the concept that a company, or an individual, has a 'place' on the **web** that can be accessed over the **internet**. Usually this means a **webpage** that is advertised by a web address (or **URL**) such as www.routledge.co.uk and this page is used to project an image of the company or individual. The web presence of an organisation may range from a very basic **welcome page** that simply advertises the organisation and lists their phone number, **email**, etc., to a more complex **homepage** that also provides a variety of **hyperlinks** to other resources and pages on the World Wide Web. The more sophisticated examples of web presence allow users to interact with the website, perhaps to purchase goods or interrogate a **database**, and often provide very useful **feedback** to the site owner. In terms of elearning, some types of **VLE** incorporate individual web pages for students to **post** their own information, photograph, etc., or may link with an individual **weblog** for students to express their own views through journal-type entries **online**.

WEBCAM

A small camera device that connects to your computer and allows video images to be transferred over the **internet** to appear as **webpages** or enable interactivity between remote users through a type of **videoconference** facility on the computer **desktop**. There are two common applications: first, to enable remote visual as well as audio **interaction** between users using a **software** service such as **Skype**, which usually requires users to have a wide **bandwidth** (e.g. **broadband**); second, webcams are used to make a particular view (e.g. a landscape or a room in a building) permanently available via a **hyperlink** on a webpage. In the latter example, some links may provide a live video image, but it is also common to transmit a still image of the scene and update this image at a regular interval of time, say every ten minutes. The use of a webcam is becoming more common in elearning as a means of providing a richer and more intimate connection with learners who are studying at a location remote from their tutor.

WEBCAST

Webcasting or netcasting refers to the streaming of audio and sometimes video over the **web**. It can also be called **internet** radio. A webcast service makes it possible to broadcast lectures, panel discussions and other events across the campus **network** and the internet. The broadcast can be live or delayed audio and/or video. For example, a university could offer **online** courses consisting of webcast lectures by the instructor or guest lecturer. Students need the appropriate **multimedia** application (for example, RealAudio) in order to view or hear the webcast. This process is referred to as 'push technology' (i.e. pushing web-based information to an internet user). Webcast **software** synchronises video, audio and slides.

The term 'streaming' is very similar to 'webcasting' and they are used interchangeably. Technically, webcasting covers all the steps in producing an online broadcast – from capture and coding of content through to delivery, whereas streaming refers to the software that actually delivers the webcast to the user's **desktop** player programme over the web. The word 'streaming' comes from the way it works: webcast data is viewed, but not actually **downloaded** in full and stored on the user's computer – it just streams through in real time, piece by piece.

There are numerous educational benefits of webcasting, and the fact that the material can be viewed live as well as stored for later use adds to the range of applications. Live broadcasts have a buzz and motivating effect for many learners, while an archive of webcasts can be reviewed, studied and made available to students for exam preparation. A course consisting primarily of webcasts is not ideal as it is hard to maintain concentration and interest in information coming from a small screen over an extended period of time. As a means of accessing a lecture from a remote expert, or to catch up on a missed lecture, or to review complex information, it can be a valuable resource.

WEBINAR

This is a name sometimes used to refer to a **virtual seminar**, or **online** seminar, included as part of a programme of **distributed education**.

WEBLOG

See: **blogging**

WEBPAGE

As its name suggests, this is a 'page' on the World Wide **Web**, usually written in **HTML** script with **hypertext** links to other pages to create a series of linked pages. A number of webpages linked together in a folder on the one computer is often called a 'website', and these are available over the **internet** when read in connection with a **web browser** or a **search engine**. The initial root location is usually referred to as the **homepage**, with subsequent links creating a large connected document, or a specialist portal linking to other webpages.

A simple webpage lists relevant information, typically in short sentences or paragraphs in order that the user does not need to scroll down too far to read detailed information. Additional information is then linked to related pages that can be 'layered' to give the user access to more detailed information, definitions, examples, etc., when required by clicking a link. One advantage of this approach is that it does not overload the user, and it allows them to self-select what they want to read or avoid (e.g. not to open large files, complex **graphics** or **audio clips**). More complex webpages contain a number of frames that can be scrolled down and searched independently or used as an easily accessible index for the website. Ideally, webpages should be designed for efficient use with a range of different web browsers – a feature that is not always observed in some of the more complex webpages.

WEBQUESTS

These are activities, using **internet** and other resources, which encourage students to use higher order thinking skills. A WebQuest is an inquiry-oriented activity in which most or all of the information used by learners is drawn from the **web**. WebQuests are designed to use learners' time well, to focus on using information rather than looking for it, and to support learners' thinking at the levels of analysis, synthesis and evaluation. WebQuests are effectively higher order learning tools. WebQuests can be combined with **blogs** and **Wikis**.

WELCOME PAGE

This is the opening screen of a **webpage** of an individual or business who has a **web presence**. The welcome page is usually also the **homepage**, though frequently welcome pages are only short, single pages, with very few additional **hyperlinks** or additional webpages. A typical welcome page might have a photograph or other **graphic**, together with an advertising statement and a list of further contacts, including phone and fax numbers, **email** address, and so on. When the welcome page is also the homepage, there will be additional links to other information on the organisation or individual and the welcome page may be used as a base to direct the user to other **online** resources.

WI-FI

Contrary to common misconception, wi-fi does not in fact refer to 'wireless fidelity'. Instead it is simply the trademarked name of the networking technology and protocols that allow computers, mobile phones, tablets and other digital devices to connect with one another, without the use of networking cables, over a designated area of wi-fi coverage.

WIKI

A Wiki (or, to use its full name, WikiWikiWeb) is group communication **software** that allows users to create and edit **webpages** very quickly using any **browser**. In fact, *wiki wiki* means 'quick' in Hawaiian. The notion of 'open editing' is what distinguishes Wikis from so much other **online** groupware. It would seem to be a recipe for chaos, and yet users all claim that chaos rarely results and, if it does, there are recovery mechanisms. This ethic at the heart of the Wiki is 'soft security', that is, it relies on the **communities**, rather than technology, to enforce order. Furthermore, the Wiki concept encourages democratic use and promotes content composition by non-technical users.

Another defining feature of Wikis is that the content is not 'owned' in the same way as conference messages. Anonymity is not required, but it is common, as a page will usually have multiple authors. The essence is group creation and refinement.

Related to open editing and group ownership is the notion of flux: links are added in and out of the page; chronology does not determine the organisation, rather the context does. A Wiki grows through accretions and links, and is constantly changing.

No programming or **HTML** knowledge is required to build a site, edit pages or create **hyperlinks** and crosslinks. Often one person or a small group of users emerges as the primary housekeeper to tidy the site and maintain a logical structure.

Unlike traditional groupware which relies on strict workflows, access restrictions and formal structures, Wikis rely on the group to make up the processes as they go along. This often leads to a very strong sense of community and group identity. As with other online communities, Wikis are a reflection of the care and attention of the users. The most obvious application of a Wiki in education is to develop writing expertise and to write joint documents. The features of the technology which support this are:

- they are fun to use;
- they are easy to use;
- they facilitate revision and refinement;
- they focus on the writing process, not the product.

Some instructors welcome the opportunity for students to develop **network** literacy in which writing for the professor is replaced by group writing in an open, collaborative environment. Wikis are also an ideal tool for group editing of documents.

WIKIPEDIA

Wikipedia is a free and **open access** encyclopaedia that is available **online** and is structured as a **Wiki**, allowing users to add to and edit the contents. From small beginnings, this service has grown to rival more conventional encyclopaedias, and it has the advantage that errors and unsubstantiated opinions can be challenged and corrected in real time, thereby keeping the resource current.

WIRELESS NETWORK

In general terms, this is any **network** that operates without cables and relies on radio communication to carry a signal. Wireless networks may support a variety of devices, including telephones, computers and personal digital assistants, usually to give users access to the **internet** or a **LAN** such as an organisational **intranet**. A wireless network may cover a single room, a building, or a wider geographical area. The advantage of a wireless connection to the internet is that it potentially allows users to go **online** from anywhere, not simply at a designated campus or learning centre. A wireless **broadband** connection offers the learner the possibility of accessing information such as a **database** or a **VLE** in the pursuit of field-based activities, and therefore extends the boundaries of the learning environment even further outside the conventional classroom. In practice, the current coverage of wireless broadband connections is geographically quite limited and places practical restrictions on the flexibility of wireless network access.

WORM

A worm is a particular type of computer **virus** that spreads by replicating itself through computer **networks** connected to the **internet**, especially by attaching themselves to **email**. Most worms do not cause real damage to a computer, unlike a **Trojan**, but they have a nuisance value similar to **spam** and waste valuable **bandwidth**. Although a good virus protection **software** hosted on a reputable **ISP** will offer a measure of protection, the ability of a worm to enter a computer connected to the internet and then send out replicas of itself to all the email addresses contained on that computer means that worms can easily be spread by users opening an email that has apparently come from a friend. The receipt of a worm is not as serious as receiving a virus, but most advice suggests that users do not open email with any suspect **attachment**.

YOUTUBE

YouTube is an **online** service which is a form of **social media**, enabling users to **post** video clips for **open access** sharing. Users can upload their own videos on a wide range of subjects (and quality standards), which can then be **tagged** and made available over the **internet**. There are many informative educational and instructional videos which can be used to extend **open education** and **heutagogy**.

XML

XML stands for 'Extensible Markup Language'. It is a text-based markup language which is used to encode documents in a form that is readable by humans and machines, and which is shareable across the **web**, other **internet** applications and any other XML-compatible applications and programmes (including many common end-user applications).

FURTHER RESOURCES

We have chosen below a selection of resources comprising books, journals, collections and organisations that will support further exploration of the key concepts, issues and approaches we have defined in this book, or which will provide practical tools and guidance for digital learning and teaching practice. This list cannot be exhaustive, but we have tried to make it balanced and representative with respect to the further sources of literature and support available in English.

Books

The following books are each highly recommended in their own right, and collectively they provide very good coverage of relevant research, scholarship, models and approaches to practice in the field of digital learning and teaching.

Beetham, H. and Sharpe, R. (Eds.) (2013). *Rethinking Pedagogy for a Digital Age* (2nd edition). New York: Routledge. A wide-ranging edited volume, with chapters from leading scholars and practitioners addressing issues including theoretical foundations, learning design, open resources, learner experiences and professional learning for educators.

Duval, E., Sharples, M. and Sutherland, R. (2017). *Technology Enhanced Learning: Research Themes*. Cham, Switzerland: Springer. An edited volume with a strong focus on theoretical issues, key literature, and research and evidence relating to dimensions including collaborative learning, virtual worlds, adaptive learning environments, self-regulated learning and digital divides.

Goodfellow, R. and Lea, M. R. (Eds.) (2013). *Literacy in the Digital University: Critical Perspectives on Learning, Scholarship and Technology*. Abingdon, Oxon: Routledge. A collection of chapters exploring academic and digital literacies in the contexts of learning and teaching, scholarship and research, further and higher education, and open practices.

Selwyn, N. (2014). *Digital Technology and the Contemporary University: Degrees of Digitization*. Abingdon, Oxon: Routledge. This book offers a thorough consideration and critique of digital technology in higher education, exploring rhetoric and reality, digital technology in relation to the organisation of universities and student and staff experiences, and possible future developments.

Weller, M. (2014). *The Battle for Open: How Openness Won and Why It Doesn't Feel like Victory*. London: Ubiquity Press. Available at: www.ubiquitypress.com/site/books/10.5334/bam/ A comprehensive exploration of digital developments in open education from one of the leading researchers and scholars in the field, and covering the areas of open access, MOOCs, open education resources and open scholarship. An open access book downloadable at the above link.

Journals

The following journals are well established in the field; between them they have published leading research, research reviews, case studies and evaluations. *IRRODL* and *Research in Learning Technology* are both open access journals offering free access to papers, with extensive archives of previous issues.

British Journal of Educational Technology

https://onlinelibrary.wiley.com/journal/14678535

Computers & Education

www.journals.elsevier.com/computers-and-education

Educational Technology Research and Development

https://link.springer.com/journal/11423

IRRODL (The International Review of Research in Open and Distributed Learning)

Open access journal available at www.irrodl.org/index.php/irrodl

Research in Learning Technology

The journal of the Association for Learning Technology. Open access journal available at www.tandfonline.com/toc/zrlt20/current

Resource collections

The Design Studio (Jisc)

The Design Studio is a collection of guidelines, resources and project outputs to support digital learning practice, produced through the activities and funded programmes of work in UK further and higher education supported by Jisc. Areas of coverage include curriculum design and development, assessment and feedback, and supporting the development of digital literacies. http://jiscdesignstudio.pbworks.com/w/page/12458422/Welcome%20to%20the%20Design%20Studio

Directory of Open Access Journals

A comprehensive, community-curated index of good-quality, peer-reviewed open access journals in a wide range of disciplines https://doaj.org/

Open Textbook Library

Supported by the Open Textbook Network in the United States, the Open Textbook Library provides access to free-to-use, open online and digital textbooks in areas including accounting and finance, business, education, maths and natural science. There are several other open textbook collections available online, so this is just one good place to start exploring.

https://open.umn.edu/opentextbooks/

Open Educational Resources Collections (EDUCAUSE)

A list of open educational resources collections produced by EDUCAUSE or their member institutions. Includes MIT OpenCourseWare (OCW) and The World Digital Library.

https://library.educause.edu/topics/teaching-and-learning/open-educational-resources-oer

OER World Map

An open education network that allows users and members to locate OER materials and resources, open education projects and initiatives, and cogent groups, practitioners and researchers who are active in the global open education community.

https://oerworldmap.org/

Organisations

Association for Learning Technology (ALT)

ALT is a UK-based association and registered charity representing institutional and individual members across all areas of the education sector. ALT provides membership services, facilitates events (including conferences), and supports networking and research through Special Interest Groups and the open access journal Research in Learning Technology. www.alt.ac.uk/

Australasian Society for Computers in Learning in Tertiary Education (Ascilite)

Similar to ALT in the UK, Ascilite is a not-for-profit membership organisation supporting networking, scholarship and research principally in Australia and New Zealand. Ascilite runs an annual conference, which is one of the major international conferences in digital learning, and publishes the open access Australasian Journal of Education Technology.

https://ascilite.org/

EDUCAUSE

EDUCAUSE is a not-for-profit association focused on the development and impact of technology in higher education. Based in the Unites States, but with a global membership of over 2300 institutions from over 40 countries, EDUCAUSE provides a range of networking, peer support, and organisational development services, and publishes research and resources for the sector.

www.educause.edu/

Jisc

A UK membership organisation that supports digital developments in education and research, through advice and consultancy, and which has also funded research and development programmes and produced various resources and resource collections for the sector (e.g. The Design Studio).

www.jisc.ac.uk/

Open Education Consortium (OEC)

A not-for-profit global membership network of institutions and organisations that are committed to supporting open education. OEC provides advocacy and leadership around the advancement of open education, to develop, find and share OER, and to develop open education policy and sustainable open education approaches and initiatives.

www.oeconsortium.org/

REFERENCES

Beetham, H. and Sharpe, R. (Eds.) (2013) *Rethinking Pedagogy for a Digital Age* (2nd edition). New York: Routledge.

Duval, E., Sharples, M. and Sutherland, R. (2017) *Technology Enhanced Learning: Research Themes*. Cham, Switzerland: Springer.

Evans, S. K., Pearce, K. E., Vitak, J. and Treem, J. W. (2017) Explicating Affordances: A Conceptual Framework for Understanding Affordances in Communication Research. *Journal of Computer-Mediated Communication*, 22, pp. 35–52.

Garrison, D. R., Anderson, T. and Archer, W. (2000) Critical Inquiry in a Text-Based Environment: Computer Conferencing in Higher Education. *The Internet and Higher Education*, 2(2–3), pp. 87–105.

Goodfellow, R. and Lea, M. R. (Eds.) (2013). *Literacy in the Digital University: Critical Perspectives on Learning, Scholarship and Technology*. Abingdon, Oxon: Routledge.

Goodyear, P. and Dimitriadis, Y. (2013) In Media Res: Reframing Design for Learning. *Research in Learning Technology*, 21, pp. 1–13.

HASTAC (n.d.) What is a digital badge? Available online at. www.hastac.org/initiatives/digital-badges

Jisc. (2016) *Curriculum Design and Support for Online Learning*. Available at: www.jisc.ac.uk/full-guide/curriculum-design-and-support-for-online-learning

Johnston, B., MacNeill, S. and Smyth, K. (2019) *Conceptualising the Digital University: The Intersection of Policy, Pedagogy and Practice*. Cham, Switzerland: Palgrave MacMillan.

Laurillard, D. (2012) *Teaching as a Design Science: Building Pedagogical Patterns for Learning and Technology*. New York: Routledge.

Prensky, M. (2001). Digital Natives, Digital Immigrants. *On the Horizon*, 9(5), pp. 1–6. https://doi.org/10.1108/10748120110424816.

Rennie, F. and Morrison, T. (2013) *e-Learning and Social Networking Handbook: Resources for Higher Education*. New York and London: Routledge.

Saadatmand, M. and Kumpulainen, K. (2013). Content Aggregation and Knowledge Sharing in a Personal Learning Environment: Serendipity in Open Online Networks. *International Journal of Emerging Technologies in Learning (iJET)*, 8, pp. 70–77. Available at: https://online-journals.org/index.php/i-jet/article/view/2362

Selwyn, N. (2014) *Digital Technology and the Contemporary University: Degrees of Digitization*. Abingdon, Oxon: Routledge.

Shukie, P. (2015) *The Big Idea: Community Open Online Courses*. Available at: www.thersa.org/discover/publications-and-articles/rsa-blogs/2015/02/the-big-ideacoocs

Siemens, G. (2005) Connectivism: A Learning Theory for the Digital Age. *International Journal of Instructional Technology and Distance Learning*, 2(1). Available at: www.itdl.org/journal/jan_05/article01.htm

Weller, M. (2011) *The Digital Scholar: How Technology Is Transforming Scholarly Practice*. Basingstoke: Bloomsbury Academic.

Weller, M. (2014) *The Battle for Open: How Openness Won and Why It Doesn't Feel like Victory*. London: Ubiquity Press. Available at: www.ubiquitypress.com/site/books/10.5334/bam/

White, D. and Le Cornu, A. (2011) Visitors and Residents: A New Typology for Online Engagement. *First Monday*, 16(9). Available at: http://firstmonday.org/ojs/index.php/fm/article/view/3171/3049

Printed in Germany
by Amazon Distribution
GmbH, Leipzig

18423470R00109